BOB MARLEY

Reggae King of the World

"How good and how pleasant it would be before God and man to see the unification of all the Africans. . ."

(Africa Unite)

POMEGRANATE ARTBOOKS ● SAN FRANCISCO

BOB MARLEY

Reggae King of the World

MALIKA LEE WHITNEY
DERMOTT HUSSEY

with foreword by RITA MARLEY

POMEGRANATE ARTBOOKS • SAN FRANCISCO

ACKNOWLEDGEMENTS

Edited by: Kim Robinson and Mike Henry
Design and Art Direction: Troy Caine
Cover Photographs: Daniel Asher
Photo Credits:

A & M Records—p. 147 (3rd from top). © Para Andy Limited—p. 13. Daniel Asher—pp. 1, 2, 8, 10, 11, 14-16, 17 (top & bottom-right), 67, 71 (bottom-left), 72 (right), 73, 86-91, 93, 94, 103, 105, 110, 119, 122 (centre & bottom), 123 (centre), 124 (top-right), 127, 129, 142, 165 (top, centre & bottom left), 169, 175, 176, 178-180, 187 (bottom), 188, 189, 191, 193, 194 (bottom), 195, 201, 204. Adrian Boot—pp. 82-83, 97. Kwame Braithwaite—pp. 113, 145 (bottom), 146 (centre & bottom), 147 (top). Astley Chin—pp. 5, 58 (top), 59, 60, 62, 64. Aston Chin—p. 54 (top). Donna Cline—p. 72 (left). Fikisha Cumbo—pp. 72-73, 77 (top), 84. Ted Cunningham (JIS)—pp. 18, 24 (top), 25, 28 (bottom), 36 (centre-left), 71 (bottom-right), 124 (top-left). Monica Dasilva—22, 34, 36 (bottom), 37 (top-left, top-right, centre-left & bottom), 40 (top), 146 (top), 173 (bottom-left & right). Dynamic Sounds—p. 13. Epic Records—p. 147 (second top). France-Soir—p. 198. Neville Garrick—pp. 131 (bottom-left), 132 (centre). Gleaner—pp. 55, 65 (top), 70, 111, 164 (bottom), 172, 177. Norman Hamilton (JTB)—p. 123 (bottom). Ossie Hamilton—pp. 38, 51, 56, 57, 75, 170. Chester Higgins—pp. 23, 29, 32, 33, 36 (right), 202-203. Island Records—pp. 71 (top-left & -right), 76, 77 (bottom), 81, 101, 137, 145 (top). Janhoi Jaja Mwenga—p. 174. Jet Magazine—p. 163 (bottom). Maria La Yacona—pp. 166, 167. Rita Marley (family collection)—pp. 40 (right), 41, 173 (top, center). David Melhado (Island Records)—p. 101. Howard Moo Young—pp. 19, 120. Keith Morrison—44, 46, 54 (bottom), 66, 78, 106, 159, 161, 168, 192. National Library of Jamaica—p. 200. Newsday—p. 98. Chuc Pulin—p. 126. Dale Robinson—pp. 182-185. Paulette Robinson—p. 196. Rockers Magazine—pp. 81, 118. Roots News Magazine—p. 17 (bottom-left). Anthony Russell (Institute of Jamaica)—p. 115. Peter Simon (Rolling Stone)p. 40 (left). Derek Smith (Nassau Tribune)—p. 194 (top). Swing Magazine—pp. 50, 58 (bottom-left), 65 (bottom). Dera Tompkins—pp. 130, 131 (top), 132 (top & bottom), 133. Karl Whitbourne—pp. 20, 26, 27, 28 (top), 30, 31, 35, 36 (top), 37 centre-right), 47, 72 (centre), 158. Zimbabwe Consulate—p. 131 (centre. Zimbabwe newspaper—p. 160.

Song lyrics:

One Love © 1982 Irving Music Inc. & Owls and Six Flies Inc. (BMI). Ambush In The Night, Babylon System, Bad Card, Crazy Baldhead, Coming In From The Cold, Exodus, Forever Loving Jah, Jamming, One Drop, Rat Race, Redemption Song, Ride Natty Ride, Running Away, So Jah Seh, Talking Blues, Time Will Tell, Wake Up And Live, Want More, We And Them, Who The Gap Fit, Zimbabwe © 1980, 1979, 1978, 1977, 1976, 1974 Bob Marley Music Ltd. (ASCAP) all rights administered by ALMO Music Corp. (ASCAP) for the world excluding the Caribbean. No Woman No Cry, Roots Rock Reggae, War © 1976, 1974 Tuff Gong Music (ASCAP) all rights administered by ALMO Music Corp. (ASCAP) for the world excluding the Caribbean. Crisis, Easy Skanking, Guiltiness, Natural Mystic, Roots, Smile Jamaica, So Much Things To Say, Three Little Birds © 1977 Bob Marley Music Ltd., controlled for U.S. & Canada by ALMO Music Corp. (ASCAP), controlled for the rest of the world excluding the Caribbean by Rondor Music Inc. I've Got To Go Home © Parandy Music Limited. All other songs © Bob Marley Music Ltd.

The authors and publishers extend their special thanks to: Andrew Henry, whose idea it was; Tuff Gong International; Neville Garrick for technical guidance, and usage of foreign press pulls and tour itinerary information; The Jamaica Daily News; Tell Precision Co. Ltd.; Osmond Watson for the reproduction of his painting "King of Hearts" on p. 112; Keith Morrison and Karl Whitbourne who generously assisted with miscellaneous visual coverage; Pearl O'Connor; Corrine Chuck; Ingrid Bryan; and Shirley Archer, Niamo Raheem, Nora Harlow, I. Jabulani Tafari, Ras Iral, Mrs. Margaret Whitney, Jahrrod Whitney, Janhoi, Nsombe, W. B. Hunt, Wemusa, Coleen Clay and Carl Gayle for guidance and support to author Whitney. Very special thanks go to Mrs. Rita Marley and Mrs. Cedella Booker, without whose support this project would never have been possible.

End Pages Illustration: Neville Garrick © 1982

Poem "Wailin" from the book *Mutabaruka: the first poems,* Paul Issa Publications Limited, © 1974, reproduced by permission

Lyrics for "Joseph" by Judy Mowatt, © 1980, reproduced by permission

© 1984 Kingston Publishers Ltd.

First Edition 1984

Second Edition 1994

ISBN 1-56640-987-X

Published by Pomegranate Artbooks, Box 6099, Rohnert Park, California 94927

Produced by Blaze International Productions, Inc., New York, N.Y.

Printed in Hong Kong

FOREWORD

Glory to Jah the Prophet has come
Give thanks and praises

("Confrontation")

Jah Live, Bob lives, his music lives—Rastafari lives forever.

Bob's last words to me were, "Rita, I am not going anywhere, I'll be with you always," and that is how it is with the whole world. Bob is with us continually.

No one can stop his music, the message is already out there. In Bob's own words, "Them a go tired to see me face, but them can't get we out of the race." Everything that I have to say pertaining to Bob, his works, his message, it's all contained in his lyrics. Bob performed for thousands of people—people of all races, colours and classes, all feeling the same vibration. All could feel that it was more than music. Whenever I saw the reactions of the people to Bob and his music, I understood the reason and purpose for all of this.

It is written, One can only know the Father through the Son and those to whom he reveal it. I and I are here to ensure that all Bob's toiling is not in vain.

One Love, One God, One Aim, One Destiny—Rastafari.

Rita Marley

CONTENTS

PREFACE

STIRRING IT UP

BY DERMOTT HUSSEY

THE EVOLUTION OF REGGAE

IN LESS THAN twenty years, Jamaica's popular music has emerged from cultural confinement. Today, in many cities around the world, reggae challenges the musical status quo.

For as long as anyone can remember, reggae's ancestor, mento, failed to get official recognition from its own people. It flourished mainly in rural Jamaica. Mento raged at country "brams", a type of lively dance or "rub-up", which were often frequented by society folk. A mento band was the focus of the country bram. These bands varied in size, but their instrumentation usually consisted of a banjo, guitar, drum, clarinet, and C melody saxophone. Meanwhile, in the busy Kingston streets of 1934, strolling musicians Slim and Sam sang at street corners with a guitar and maracas. Their lyrics were risqué, topical and sold for a pretty penny. But mento songs were more pre-meditated than their Trinidadian counterparts, the calypsoes, in their play on words.

Mento's basic beat shows a predominantly African influence. In addition, it has a Spanish tinge; a doubling bass figure and a rhythmic sound that is a cross between a rhumba and a beguine. No one is altogether sure of the origins of this Latin flavour; it might have appeared in the music when Jamaican labourers migrated to Cuba in the 1920s to work on sugar plantations, or possibly when many Cubans settled in Jamaica in the late thirties.

Mento, as a rural dance or street music, was frowned on by middle Jamaica. It was not played in the polite drawing rooms of St. Andrew, for it was the people's music. The music achieved a slight breakthrough into high society in the late forties when a colourful singer with the royal name of "Lord Fly" sang it in a fashionable midtown Kingston club, The Colony. Fly, it is said, cleaned up the suggestive lyrics for the patrons. In the early hours, however, when only the hardcore fans remained he delved into the vernacular. His explorations in mento and calypso inspired other singers like Harold Richardson and the Ticklers, and Lord Messam.

Fly's great rival was the brilliant and self-styled "Lord Flea", an unsung hero who, it is said, influenced Harry Belafonte's Jamaican folk songs and calypsoes of the fifties. Mento was also fused successfully with calypso and with the subsequent active support of the visitor industry, the mento band mistakenly became known as the calypso band, a misnomer that persists until this day. In the 1940s mento was recorded by a pioneer studio, Stanley Motta, in the 78 format, thus reflecting its creeping success. It began to wane in popularity as migration and urbanization began to affect the Jamaican population. And so by 1956 only a handful of its exponents were actively recording music, and this only for the tourist trade and a small local audience. As mento music fell away so rhythm and blues began to rise in its place—the measure of the two giving a common basis to the subsequent forms of ska, rock steady and reggae.

Mento was no match for the onslaught of imported American pop records at a time when limited recording facilities existed in Jamaica and there was continuous music from radio stations in Memphis, Tennessee, and WINZ Miami, whose signals were picked up all over the island. The early rhythm and blues had the people dancing to Louis Jordan's hit "Choo Choo Chi Boogie", to the music of Roscoe Gordon, Fats Domino and Amos Milburn. Noticeably rhythm and blues was like mento, in its stressing of what is an African-derived musical trait, the after-beat, where the syncopation comes on the second and fourth beats.

Almost overnight, a new breed of Jamaican entertainer sprang up, the legendary "sound system" man, forerunner to the disc jockey. Equipped with heavy watt amplifiers and huge speakers that required trucking to locations, the "systems" men hired halls like Jubilee and Forrester in the Kingston ghetto. While selling liquor and playing a mix of jazz and R&B hits, the "systems" men became battling musical warlords. And men like Duke Reid, Sir Coxsone, Tom Sebastian and Prince Buster controlled their territories by subduing them with thundering bass frequencies that petrified dance hall crowds; further afield, the sound carried on the still night air for two miles and more, making it hard for other citizens to get some sleep.

As time passed the battle narrowed to Coxsone and the late Duke Reid. Coxsone would visit Miami, rummage a record shop for an obscure R&B hit and return with the label scratched off in order to hide the origin of the label, the singer, and the song from his rival. The music, very often retitled by Coxsone, drew the crowd with its exclusivity. Reid, undaunted, would go into the studio with an aspiring group of local musicians and record a cover version of a popular song on soft wax, and possibly an original which was sold to "systems" men in neighbouring territories with smaller reputations. This facility allowed early singers like Owen Grey, Laurel Aitken and Jackie Edwards, as well as Bunny and Scully, to come to the fore. Through the "systems" men they gained a popularity that not even the radio station could offer since they were predominantly occupied with imported music, a charge that is still laid against them today.

Jamaican R&B versions emulated the New Orleans sound of tenor saxes, trumpets, trombones, boogie piano, and the instrument that is most crucial to the music, the bass. Its influence became heavier, and by the early sixties the records began to feature the shuffle rhythm accentuated by the brass section riffing on the off beat. The sound of that riff was called ska.

Ska was an exciting big band sound, unlike anything heard today. Essentially an instrumental music, it had a limited vocal accompaniment in which Prince Buster, Delroy Wilson, Justin Hinds and the Dominoes, and Toots and the Maytals excelled themselves behind the chugging straight ahead beat. However, the true masters of the form were the members of a brilliant band, The Skatalites. It was a short-lived band (1964-1965) of iconoclasts, but during their tenure they turned out a music that embodied the best of what had gone before and which, in a sense, became the summation of an era. The band consisted of Tommy McCook, tenor sax; Roland Alphonso, tenor sax; Lester Sterling, alto sax; Johnny Moore, trumpet; Don Drummond, trombone; Jackie Mittoo, piano; Lloyd Brevett, bass; Lloyd Knibbs, drums; and Jah Jerry Hines, guitar.

Some of the best ska tunes were based on the classic call and response pattern, which is at the root of Jamaican work songs and Rastafari* sectarian preaching, where the soloists make statements against the framework of an answering chorus. A significant number of the musicians who made up the Skatalites and bands before them came from a background of dispiriting poverty; some were the products of poor broken homes, some were orphans, and most came from Alpha's Boys Band, a legendary school band with a tradition of nearly 100 years. Four members of the Skatalites came from Alpha—Drummond, McCook, Sterling and Moore.

In the beginning the Skatalites played a few engagements in rural Jamaica before doubling as producer Clement Dodd's great studio band, and the best dance band of its kind, which was housed at the Bournemouth Bathing Club. Not only did they play their own compositions, but also cover versions of pop tunes selected by Dodd.

* Rastafari: movement that recognizes His Imperial Majesty Emperor Haile Selassie as the Black Messiah.

The singular talent of the period was the trombonist and tragic figure, Don Drummond. His musical vision of minor blues and uncommon harmonies, is today, twelve years after his death, still unsurpassed. His personality was that of the brooding perfectionist musician whose Rastafari sensibilities struggled against insanity while he created original music, all of which made him a truly romantic figure. Drummond's "Marcus Garvey Junior", "Fidel", "Johnn Dark", "Man in the Street", and "Addis Ababa", were forerunners to the upsurg of black consciousness in the late sixties and a driving spirit for his musical successor, Bob Marley.

From 1963 onwards, the tempo of fast moving ska slowed down for fundamen changes. A vocal music evolved from th instrumental preoccupations of ska. With the break-up of the Skatalites in 1965 and the subsequent death of Don Drummond, an era was firmly at an end. The new music was called rock steady.

Rhythmically, the emphasis was changed from straight 4/4 to the drummer accenting between the second and the fourth beat. The bass, the bedrock of reggae, became more focal and its melodic side was emphasized. The new music required less horns, reflecting the economic factor that horns were more expensive. Songwriter singers became dominant. Many rose up, individual talents like Alton Ellis, Delroy Wilson, Bob Andy, Hopeton Lewis and Ken

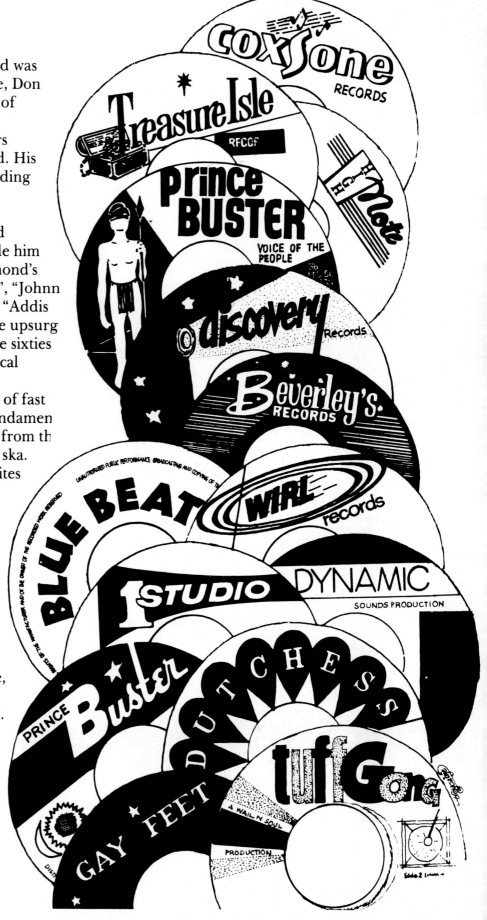

A CORNUCOPIA OF JAMAICA'S MUSICAL HISTORY . . .

Above: some of the earliest record labels which featured many of the hit tunes from the late 50s to the mid-60s. Some have undergone changes, some are now defunct and a few are still around today. Opposit page: some of the popular musical giants of the early years. From top: (L-R) Don Drummond, Duke Reia V-Rocket (sound system operator), The Skatalites, Toots & The Maytals, Desmond Dekker, Carlos Malco Jackie Opel, Bob Andy, Derrick Morgan, Ken Boothe, Jackie Edwards, Byron Lee, Lord Tanamo, Theophilus Beckford, Hortense Ellis, Derrick Harriott, Alton Ellis, The Blues Busters, Millie Small, Delroy Wilson and young Bob Marley.

12

Boothe; groups, like the Heptones, the Melodians and Justin Hinds and the Dominoes.

The Rastafari and "Rude Boy"* sentiments of protest and rage that were instrumentalized by Drummond and the Skatalites, took a lyrical form. Political protest by song became popular while other songs continued to speak of the people's hardship.

There is no gladness
Nothing but sadness
Nothing like a pinch of meal
I've got to leave this land
I just can't stand this life I'm living

(Bob Andy—
"I've Got To Go Back Home")

Despite the serious lyric concerns, rock steady was essentially a dance music, offering the participant less vigorous involvement than ska. It was more laid back, giving rise to "renting a tile", a style of dance where movement is restricted to marking time on the spot, and resolving one's frustrations there.

The popularity of the music stimulated the old producer rivalry once again between Coxsone, Duke Reid and newcomer Leslie Kong of Beverly's Records. The mighty Coxsone, however, was always a step ahead of his competitors whether it was during the ska or rock steady periods, and his claim that reggae

* Rude Boys: movement of young toughs prevalent in the sixties.

13

began in his studio is as close to the truth as any. It is said that while preparing for a session with engineer Ivan Morris some time in 1968, session guitarist Eric Frater played a guitar strum through a newly acquired echo phaser and reggae's guitar strum was born.

The new music combined all the styles which had gone before, but with a spiritual content only partially evident during the rock steady period. The growing Rastafarian faith gave the music a new urgency, a new spirit. And stylistically the sound of the group led by Bob Marley—The Wailers—became the definitive universal sound.

The musical assurance of The Wailers sprang from a depth of experience, in a continuum that began in the early sixties. The original Wailing Wailers was formed at this time. The group consisted of Bob Marley on rhythm guitar, Peter

Tosh on lead guitar, Bunny Livingston on percussion, and Junior Braithwaite on bass, with a vocal back-up of two female singers.

Meanwhile, Aston "Family Man" Barrett, bassist, and his brother Carlton, a drummer, formed a band in Eastern Kingston in the mid-sixties called the Hippy Boys. As well as both Barretts, it had Reggie on rhythm guitar, Payne Adams—keyboards and Webby—lead guitar. They mainly did shows, but the two brothers also recorded as the Upsetters, playing sessions at the leading studios.

During the years 1968, 1969, and 1970 they backed Bob Marley and his group, and in 1972 it was decided that the Wailers and the Upsetters would come together as one group under the name of the Wailers. The group visited Britain to negotiate contracts with Chris Blackwell before returning to Jamaica to record the first album, *Catch A Fire*. The band at the time consisted of Bob Marley on rhythm guitar, Peter Tosh—lead guitar, Bunny Livingston—percussion, Earl "Wire" Lindo—keyboards, Aston Barrett—bass, and Carlton Barrett on drums. From then on, it was success all the way.

It was as if the people had entrusted their consciousness to the Wailers. They raised the life in Trench Town, Kingston 12, to the forefront of awareness in Jamaica and internationally, inspiring the American poet Gil Scott-Heron to sing of reggae as a storm music beating in the bush and bouncing off the concrete walls in the ghetto of the world. This is surely evidence that Bob Marley's music set a standard by which all else will be judged for a long time to come■

Che MARLEY UPRISING

ROBERT NESTA MARLEY, O.M.,* also known as "Gong", was "Tuff Gong", the big bad one, the boss, as the expression implies. A street poet who became a legend in his own time, and one of the world's most important musical talents of the 1970s.

Marley was an important songwriter; he wrote of his personal life with such intensity and emotion that he often drew fresh pictures from what had already been a common experience shared by many people.

> **No sun will shine in my day today**
> **The high yellow moon won't come out to play**
> **I say darkness has covered my life light**
> **And has changed my day into night**
> **Where is the love to be found**
> **Won't someone tell me 'cause life must be somewhere around**
> **Instead of Concrete Jungle where the living is hardest**
> **Man you've got to do your very best**
>
> ("Concrete Jungle")

He was more than that too. Rastaman, a "Wailer" crying out for righteousness and justice, for as he once said, "Anyone who cry out for righteousness and justice is a wailer." He has been seen by many who knew him as a latter day prophet in the tradition of Marcus Garvey whom he has surpassed in popularity, since the song can communicate the word more effectively than the word can itself. Throughout his career Marley expressed the consciousness of the black poor, as well as that of those who were poor, but not necessarily black.

Raised on hard times and hungry living, Bob Marley never became embittered by the permanent trauma of poverty. He turned hard times into a steely defiance and a zeal to succeed no matter what the odds. From the very beginning his songs expressed his most passionate concerns.

* O.M.: Order of Merit, third highest honour awarded by the Government of Jamaica.

I'm a rebel, soul rebel
I'm a capturer, soul adventurer . . .

("Soul Rebel")

The structure of the reggae song owes much to his stewardship. The sing-talk style, for example, where Marley conducts call-and-response with himself, is a technique he used many times. In a moment of social criticism, his dialect speech in "Hypocrites" is on target. Again, in the classic "Duppy Conqueror", he is defiant but more spiritually assertive.

The bars could not hold me
Walls could not hold me
They tried to keep me down
But God is still around

("Duppy Conqueror")

In his evolution from Rude Boy, Soul Rebel, Revolutionary, into Rastaman, he produced rich examples of his song craft, demonstrating his stature as folk poet; he translated the people's feelings into poems of social comment, protest and spiritual belief, in a manner which the people themselves could probably never equal, but with which they would certainly agree.

Marley's impact was more than musical. This was clearly demonstrated at the Peace Concert of April 1978 in Jamaica, a live performance which musically was not one of his best but certainly one of his most profound, when he brought then Prime Minister, Mr. Michael Manley, and the Leader of the Opposition, Mr. Edward Seaga, together on stage, an extraordinary gesture for any pop artist to make, let alone in the strife-torn political atmosphere of Jamaica at that time.

Marley's world-wide popularity put Jamaica on the map like never before, superseding the association which Harry Belafonte had had with the island when he recorded his first songs about Jamaica a decade earlier. The portrayal of Bob's Rastafarian beliefs in some of his music lifted the movement from the level of an indigenous Jamaican religion to that of an international phenomenon, and his reference to the Bible and its wisdom, its present day revelations, brought a prophetic ring to his message and his music. The message has awakened the consciousness of people in some of the remotest places, and for recognition of his work he was the premier performer at the Independence Celebrations of Zimbabwe in April 1980. Meanwhile, among black American audiences, where reggae had long been said to have little appeal, Marley gained considerable ground in his later years, particularly with his last album, which caused his close friend and admirer Stevie Wonder to record a tribute song entitled "Master Blaster".

Marley's death signalled the end of an era. It was he more than any other who pushed Jamaica's music out from cultural confinement into a much vaster dimension; where he became the voice of the Third World. His passing also meant that his kind of reggae went with him, but the legacy of his albums, including those as yet unreleased, will ensure that he remains the undisputed master of reggae.

JAMAICA

CAPITAL: Kingston

LARGEST CITIES & TOWNS: Kingston, Montego Bay, Spanish Town, May Pen, Savanna-la-Mar, Mandeville, Port Antonio, St. Ann's Bay, Morant Bay, Ocho Rios.

LOCATION: Situated in the centre of the Caribbean Sea, 77° W and 18° N, 90 miles south of Cuba and 310 miles off the coast of Honduras. Jamaica is the 3rd largest island in the Caribbean.

CLIMATE: Warm all year round with an annual average temperature of 80°F. The coolest months are November to April.

ELEVATION: Highest: 7,402 ft. (2,256 metres) (Blue Mountain Peak). Lowest: Sea level. Over 60% of the country is over 1,000 ft.

LONGEST RIVERS: Rio Minho (Clarendon)—57 miles, Black River (St. Elizabeth)—44 miles.

MAJOR PRODUCTS: Bauxite, Sugar, Coffee, Rum, Bananas, Pimento, Alumina, Citrus. Jamaica is the world's largest producer and second largest exporter of bauxite. Tourism is a large foreign exchange earner.

FORM OF GOVERNMENT: Independent parliamentary democracy with an elected Parliament (60 members) and a nominated Upper House—Senate (21 members). A well-established two-party system with General Election every 5 years. Voting age—18 years and over.

PRINCIPAL LANGUAGE: English

PRINCIPAL RELIGIONS: Protestant, Roman Catholic, Ethiopian Orthodox, Muslim.

HISTORY: Originally inhabited by Arawak Indians, the island was "discovered" by Christopher Columbus in 1494. Spain colonised it in 1509 and lost it to the English in 1655 who held it as a crown colony for 307 years until Monday, August 6, 1962 when the island became independent.

NATIONAL MOTTO: "Out of Many, One People"

MONETARY UNIT: Jamaican Dollar.

MUSIC: Home of world-famous Reggae which succeeded Rock Steady (late 60s) and Ska (early 60s)—all of which have distinct traits of Mento which is derived from the country's African ancestry.

MEMBER OF THE UNITED NATIONS.

LEGEND

- – – – – Parish Boundaries
- ——— Main Roads
- +++++++ Railways
- ⊙ Cities and Towns
- ● Points of Interest
- ● Bauxite-producing Areas

AREA: 4,411 sq. miles (11,400 sq. km)
WORLD RANK: 144th.
POPULATION: 2,500,000
WORLD RANK: 114th

Both Marcus Garvey and Bob Marley originated in the parish of St. Ann which is dubbed Jamaica's "Garden Parish"—as also are popular recording artistes Ernie Smith, Burning Spear and ska stars Justine Hinds and The Dominoes.

Feeling out, feeling down
This feeling wouldn't leave me alone
Then up came one that said
Hey dread, hey dread, fly natty dread
And smile—you're in Jamaica
Come on and smile in Jamaica
Get it together y'all, in Jamaica
Get it together now, in Jamaica
Soulful town, soulful people
Said I see you are having fun
Dancing to the reggae ridim
O island in the sun—smile
We're gonna help our people
Help them right, O Lord help us tonight
Cast away the evil spell
Pour some water in the well and smile . . .
Ridimwise, dubwise and otherwise

Can't criticise, so smile
Help my people, help them right
O Lord help us tonight
Cast away the evil spell
Pour some water in the well and smile . . .

INTRODUCTION

PICTURE POSTCARDS with inscriptions like "Having a wonderful time, wish you were here," have travelled the world over, spouting the wondrous beauty of the year-round sun-kissed island of Jamaica. God's country. A place where happy tourists have packed away their cares and woes for a brief respite to savour its scintillating waters, beautiful beaches, blue mountain backdrop and friendly people.

But there are many other frames that in a camera's eye would send these same sun seekers packing. High unemployment, inadequate housing, and limited educational facilities, for example. Jamaica's inhabitants are a rainbow of people in mosaic mixtures that have, nonetheless, meshed into a canvas of what life is all about—living.

Jamaica, with a past, a present and future that couldn't happen anywhere else, land of wood and water, birthplace of heroes.

Birthplace of Bob Marley, one of the country's brightest stars. The Honourable Robert Nesta Marley, O.M., Reggae King of the World, who through his thought-provoking and emotionally gripping musical commentary has allowed the peoples of the earth to acknowledge their common bonds and work for change.

Bob Marley, the Rastaman who emerged from the ghetto to become a contemporary Griot, with the ability to put things in a musical perspective for reference now and always.

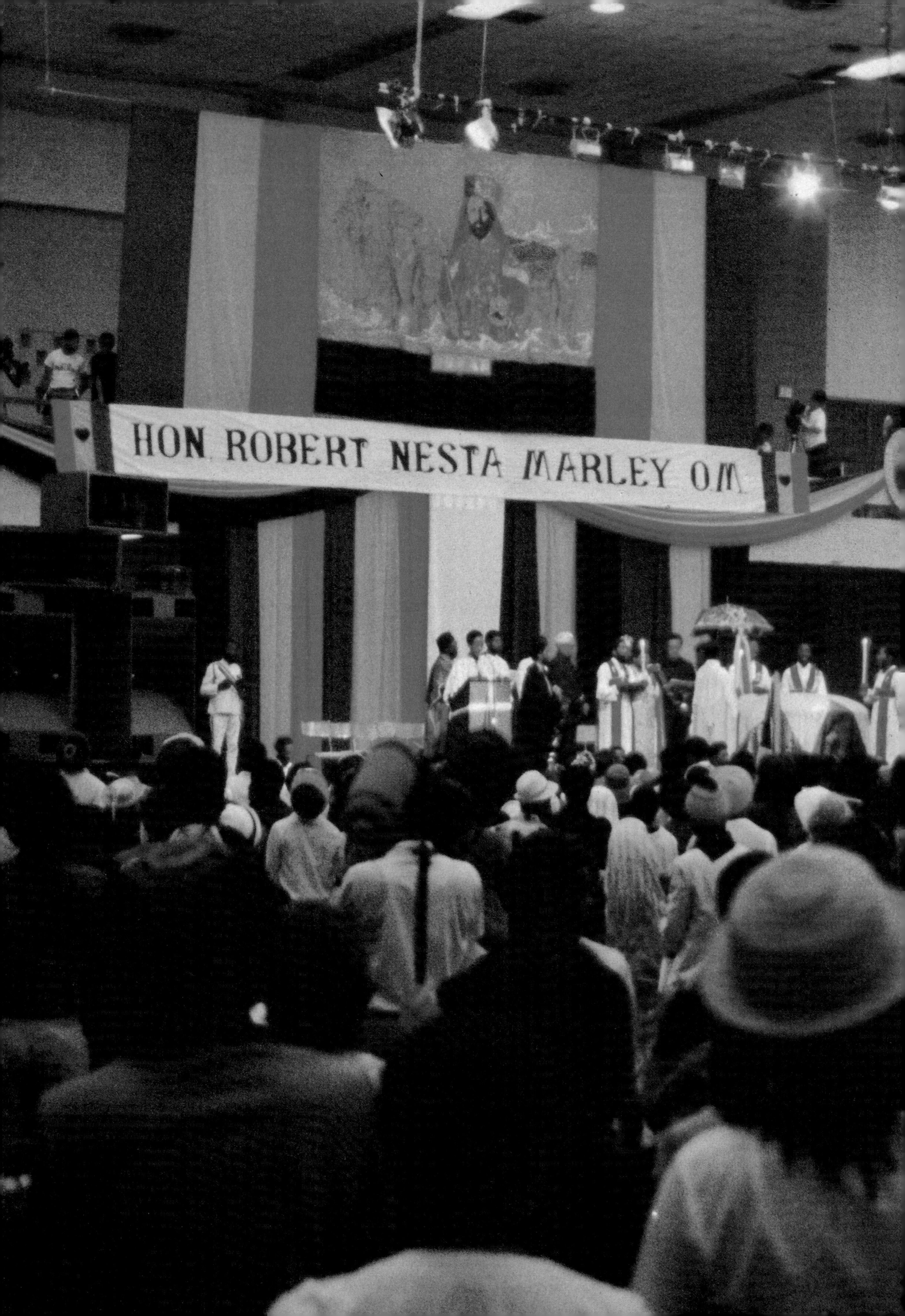
HON ROBERT NESTA MARLEY O.M.

CHAPTER I

EXODUS

Every man has the right to decide his
own destiny
And in this judgement there is no
partiality

("Zimbabwe")

N THE MORNING of May 11, 1981 at the age of thirty-six, Robert Nesta Marley chose Zion.*

You think it's the end
But it's just the beginning . . . .

("Want More")

Bob Marley. To many he was a singer, to some he was a saint. With his lyric litany he attacked those forces who were most responsible for the social conditions in which he lived, and dared to ask them why. He provoked a conscious awareness among people all over the world and encouraged them to take stock of themselves and to make whatever adjustments to their lifestyles that were necessary.

On the morning of May 21, 1981, they all came to pay their respects, the well-heeled and the barefoot. They had filed in numbers like the stones in the Great Wall of China. For three days the procession seemed endless. Some were moving motionless, ignoring the urgings of the uniformed, past the golden-hued encasement where Bob Marley's mortal flesh was taking time out.

*Zion: the Promised Land.

The rituals performed were ancient; from the first civilization of Africa, from the first named Ethiopia. The incense of frankincense and myrrh permeated the walls of the headquarters of the Ethiopian Orthodox Church on Maxfield Avenue, and blended with the smell of fresh hot peanuts outside the National Arena. Marley was still rendering assistance to his people: it was a good day for the street vendors.

In close consultation with his family, the Jamaican government stepped in to give Marley a national funeral befitting a man who had given of himself and was now stepping out. But what a paradox, Bob might have remarked, knowing that the average man in the street could hardly afford to buy his records, while the government's scheduled debate on the budget for the entire nation of Jamaica was postponed for this national period of mourning. That same government, whose amassed energy was mostly consumed by a raucous banging of chairs during parliamentary proceedings for ratification of what becomes the law of the land, was now belatedly channeling

> *"Hypocrite and parasite*
> *Will come up and take a bite*
> *And if night should turn to day*
> *A lot of people would run away . . ."*
> **(Who The Cap Fit)**

that energy in a rush to pin a medal on the man who had already been decorated by JAH.*

Marley was awarded the Order of Merit, the nation's third highest honour. There were many who argued that this was a token and that their superstar deserved more. Some said less.

**A good man is never honoured in his own land
Nothing strange, nothing's changed.**

("Survival")

Inside the National Arena the appropriate draped colours of black, green and gold for the nationhood blended with the red, gold and green of the brotherhood and sisterhood of Rastafari. A multitude of The Twelve Tribes of Israel in all their regalia reflected an "ital"** kaleidoscope. Outside, speaker boxes blared more earplay than reggae music had ever been afforded in a single dose on Jamaican radio. And among the many who came, ironically some were those who had previously turned a deaf ear to Bob's music.

*Jah: Rastafarian word for God, abbreviated from "Jehovah".   **ital: Rastafarian word meaning vital, natural, pure.

*"Woe to the downpressor
They eat the bread of sad tomorrow . . ."*
(Guiltiness)

*"Babylon system is the vampire
Sucking the blood of the sufferers . . ."*
(Babylon System)

Top: Bob's body lying in state at the Ethiopian Orthodox Church, Maxfield Avenue, Kingston. Right: insignia of the Order of Merit, Jamaica's third highest honour which was awarded to Bob. Below: one of the special Jamaican postage stamps issued by the Postmaster General in honour of the King. Opposite: Bob's family solemnly heads the large congregation awaiting the start of funeral proceedings at the National Arena.

24

Now that Bob had been physically unplugged, they wanted to listen or at least to appear to. Some were in three-piece suits with solemnity pasted on their faces. People from whom Bob Marley could not get the time of day during his lifetime were now lionizing him. Some were there to see and be seen.

> **But me no have no friends inna high society**
> **Me no have no friends, oh mark my identity**
> **Me no have no friends . . . .**

("We And Them")

It seemed a day mostly for the privileged; a special ticket was required to get in. But the real vibrations came from the common people. The sister and the brother on the street. Those who stood between the tweeters of the drum and bass business that Marley's music message was all about.

> **There's a natural mystic flowing through the air**
> **If you listen carefully now you will hear**
> **It may be the first trumpet**
> **Might as well be the last**
> **Many more will have to suffer**
> **Many more will have to die**
> **Don't ask me why**

("Natural Mystic")

The foundations of differences were undermined for this special time when all were united in their recognition of the importance of this great achiever.

Before the casket was closed, Mrs. Rita Marley made a burnt offering, carefully placing a stalk of sensemilia inside, which would enable Bob to sing once again, "excuse me while I light my spliff . . ."

The nation's flag of black, green and gold was stretched across in independent support of one of Jamaica's favoured sons. And during the service, there was an intense feeling that Bob was standing at the door watching the whole affair, that at any moment he would just belt out a loud Y—E—A—H!

The Twelve Tribes of Israel reflect the dignity and the panorama of the funeral (below). Above: the Abuna presides over the ceremony. Opposite page: (clockwise) Allan "Skill" Cole reads text, Mrs. Cedella Booker gives a mother's tribute, The I Threes pay their tribute and Bob's sons Steve and Ziggy add their touch to the occasion.

"Today we are all gathered here from different parts of the world to share our love and respect for our Brother Berhane Selassie (Light of The Trinity), the Hon. Bob Marley who has fallen asleep. But we can be comforted with the knowledge of a glorious resurrection for all and hope of eternal life to them who have fallen asleep in Christ."
(His Eminence Abuna Yesehaq Archbishop of The Ethiopian Orthodox Church In The Western Hemisphere)

"His music did more than entertain. He translated into music, in a remarkable style, the aspirations, pain and feeling of millions of people throughout the world. As an individual, Bob Marley was the embodiment of discipline and he personified hard work and determination to reach his goals. He left us with a rich heritage of popular Jamaican music."

(Prime Minister Edward Seaga)

"He was a genius. He's one of those extraordinary figures that . . . comes along perhaps once in a generation; who, starting with a folk art, a folk form, by some inner magic of commitment, sincerity of passion and of just skill, turns it into a part of the universal language of the arts of the world."

(Former Prime Minister Michael Manley)

We gonna chase those crazy
   baldheads outta the town
I and I build the cabin
I and I plant the corn
Didn't my people before me
Slave for this country
Now you look at me with scorn
Then you eat up all my corn

("Crazy Baldheads")

The proceedings continued; some were entertained whilst others received inner attainment, lamenting and reflecting. The service was beamed live via satellite, printed, shown and played during prime time throughout the world, everything from Allan "Skill" Cole's detour from the official planned scripture readings to Bob's eldest son Ziggy's jumping, jiving jig.

A swarm of international journalists and photographers, some of whom may have once filled their news reports with stories about what they referred to as Rastafarian riff raff, were now elbowing for the best vantage point to record the last important event in the life of the front line man.

So the world watched, still stunned at the loss of so great a man, still unable to come to grips with his transition, though they had been warned of it some eight months previously. It had been reported, shortly after the September 1980 Madison Square Garden concert in

New York, that Marley had collapsed while jogging in Central Park with "Skill" Cole (top rated Jamaican footballer and one of Marley's long time companions) and a few others from the constant entourage. "Skill" had always encouraged Marley to keep in peak physical form, and whenever the two got together they would jog or play Marley's favourite sport, soccer.

"Skill" recalled the tragic incident in an interview with author Whitney.

MLW: Could you describe that fateful day in September 1980?

SC: We were playing football with some others and we move go leave them and start to jog. We stop and wait for the rest of them to come up and we start to walk a little and we were about two hundred yards from them and a couple of people was behind and then all of a sudden me see Bob start shake and turn and start point to the sky and him say "Allan, Allan" and me think [it was something he was showing me] so I look in the sky and I look [at] the man and I see the man twist and start to shake and I say something wrong. Then I see

him go back and him say "Allan, Allan" and speech was leaving him. So me lift him up now and take off him track top and make a pillow and put him on the ground and foam start to come out his mouth and a bredren* come and hold him hand and squeeze it and he was getting speechless and him colour start to change. That go on for almost a minute, it come like a man have epi-

*bredren: literally "brethren", or in this case, "brother".

The great multitude rises, salutes and throngs Bob's casket as it is ushered slowly out of the National Arena after the funeral service.

leptic fits. Me get frighten and me ask him if this is the first time this happen and him tell me yeah, so me say you better get a check-up tomorrow, and that was a Sunday evening after the Madison Square Garden Concert in New York.

MLW: Was Bob checked in immediately after the seizure?

SC: Him never check in, we just go to a neurologist and other top doctors. The doctors spoke to me and say this case look serious.

MLW: Was Bob coherent when he went to the doctors, able to speak and such?

SC: Yeah man. Him say boy me no understand this and the doctor say him don't have more than 17 days to live and me no want to accept that. I understand what the doctor say in terms of medical science, the neurologist say that [Bob had a brain tumour].

As the King returns home— multitudes jam the roadways and village squares (above and right) for a glimpse of the motorcade.

In the public's mind the Madison Square Garden concert was the last performance, but in fact the Wailers did go on to perform in Pittsburgh. To many witnesses Bob was a shadow of his former shaman self on stage. Following this, Marley checked into Cedars of Lebanon Hospital in Miami and then moved from there to Sloan Kettering Hospital in New York.

Malignant melonoma was the lethal arsenal attacking the cells that had sidelined the messenger, who was about to take his team to conquer the important audience in North America. Marley had wanted to replace some of the meaningless meanderings of funk and disco with a toke of real roots. Unfortunately, the remainder of the "Uprising" tour was cancelled.

The family, "Skill" and Dr. Carl "Pee Wee" Fraser (one of Marley's personal physicians) then sought the expertise of Dr. Josef Issels from Germany who was lecturing at the American Cancer Society in New York. Dr. Issels is noted for his unorthodox treatment methods and for attempting to reverse what appears to be a hopeless case with some success. The doctor agreed to admit Marley to his private clinic in the Bavarian Alps in West Germany. Marley was rushed there by Concorde. Dr. Issels began a series of treatments that postponed the inevitable. Purification and cleansing of the body, a very strict diet and no herbs plus the wonder drug Interferon was the "Rx".

It is said that Marley's "majestic" locks eventually succumbed to the chemotherapy treatment (though some people believe that they were cut off), as the dread cancer continued to play hopscotch, jumping from his brain to his liver and lungs. Yet his condition improved—after a few months he was able to walk for up to 1½ hours in the mountains. But although the cancer retreated from many areas in his body, the brain tumour remained. Then came a setback: Marley began to accumulate a lot of fluid in his lungs, and Dr. Issels was forced to acknowledge defeat. Marley was discharged, and began the journey back to Jamaica. In Miami he became too ill to travel any further. He was re-admitted to the Cedars of Lebanon Hospital, where he died.

* * *

I'm going to prepare a place that where I am
Thou shall abide . . . .

("So Jah Seh")

As the funeral cortege assembled and caterpillared its way along the winding road, the mood became sombre. Bob Marley's mortal flesh was returning to the village of his birth to rest. The previously announced route was lined with people confirming that "Jah Lives," and paying homage by expressing brief thoughts aloud while long lasting feelings remained within.

The journey was long and arduous. At one point the hearse broke down and had to transfer its passenger to another vehicle. By the time most people reached the sleepy hamlet, the brief ceremony at the specially built mausoleum had been concluded. Those who really wanted to communicate more deeply with Bob Marley stayed on, mingling with the simple folk they had met along the way.

One intimate gesture of praise was paid by Nigerian percussionist Babatunde Olatunji, who played traditional African ceremonial bells in preparation for Marley's departure from Babylon* and arrival in Zion.

People at the interment thought nothing of kissing or collecting in hero worship some of the very earth where Marley was buried. Many mourned Marley's transition, but others knew that this was not the end. Sister Judy Mowatt of the I-Threes (the Wailers' backing singers) summed up that knowledge in an interview with author Whitney.

> *"They should have known*
> *Jamaica was his home born ground*
> *Instead of flying the sick man up and*
> * down*
> *They should have known*
> *That in Jamaica there's Bush Doctor*
> *Spring from out of the soil*
> *Straight from Africa . . ."*
> (*I Come To See Bob Marley, Marley Gone Away*
> F. Toots Hibbert, February '82
> © Rydim Music [Island Music])

MLW: When it became apparent that Bob was imminently about to transcend, how did that knowledge affect you?

JM: Well, we know that we are not here to stay in this temple forever, because the Bible tells us that we are here for a time. We are in this world but we are not of this world but of the world to come, so we know that the Bible tells us that we shall be changed from mortality to immortality. From corruption which is when the flesh takes on a lot of sins to incorruption. So we know that we are here to fulfill a particular work and whenever that time has expired then you are going to travel on into another world, to make a transition into that world which God has promised to his children. Well, physically it is hard to accept the fact that [Bob] has passed because it means that we wouldn't

*Babylon: Rastafarian reference to this evil world.

...ea of people converge on ...knoll at Nine Miles, St. ...n (above), through which ...s. Rita Marley (left) leads ...casket and entourage up ...he hill-top mausoleum ...re Bob will be laid to rest.

see him again in this flesh, in this life, but in knowing the Creator and his intelligence, his promises, his reassurance, you know that we shall meet again in the new Jerusalem. And I am positive that if I have gotten the chance to go to Mount Zion as my work would permit me, I know that I will see my brother again. So sometimes it will hit me because I know that physically you must think about it and there are a lot of things to reminisce about, but what I have to strengthen me is his philosophy which I am trying to live. That is what I am trying my best to continue, living it for myself. When I know that I can live it for myself, I can invite others to do the same through my songs.

I never stop singing redemption songs because that is what [Bob] asked of everyone, to help me sing songs of freedom because all I ever had was redemption songs, and this is what I think that most of us are doing, are striving after, to upgrade standards [so] that wherever he is he knows, because it is not that he can't see, it is just that we cannot communicate physically again. You can communicate in a vision. When you are in a vision, [it is] spirit and spirit [that] communicate. And even if we do not get a vision, we know that he sees everything that happens and he

Some climbed trees . . . some climbed each other (top), all to witness the final departure of the casket into the mausoleum (opposite page, bottom) which stands proudly beside the little old house, now renovated, where Bob grew up and spent his humble rural days. (See opposite page centre right—house prior to renovation.) Many who can still recall adventures of the young Bob, like the couple above, found themselves rubbing shoulders with famous celebrities such as American recording star Roberta Flack (centre left) at the King's funeral.

wants to know that he can get that self-gratification, that his work was not in vain. It lives through people. It lives through you and it lives through me. By you accepting; and I myself as a singer can still transcend his message to one and one. Once the work that he was sent to do was done then we know that that is an obedient soldier unto the Almighty and we know that a man will get paid according to his work, so I definitely know as a fact that Bob is right in the bosom of Abraham with all the saints that have passed for this cause, I know he is with them now doing a higher form of work because [it] is like a graduation from one class to another, so he is there now performing the work, still in the spiritual realms with the angels and the saints.

CHAPTER 2

THE ROOTS

Some are leaves, some are branches
But I, I, I are the root

("Roots")

ROBERT NESTA MARLEY wailed his first cry into the world on February 6, 1945. A simple wood frame house in the hilltop hamlet of Rhoden Hall, situated in a remote area of St. Ann, one of Jamaica's most beautiful parishes, was the venue.

At Rhoden Hall, the rugged hills are lushly wooded, and during its mostly misty mornings, a spectacular sunrise opens the day. Resting on the mountainside, the village is small. A place where time passes slowly. The people are close to the soil and God-fearing. Cedella Booker, Bob's mother, was born there.

Rise up this morning
Smile with the rising sun
Three little birds
Sit by my doorstep. . . .

("Three Little Birds")

According to Mrs. Booker, Bob's father, Norval Sinclair Marley, was born in Clarendon, an adjacent parish. Mrs. Booker relates that he was the overseer of a large ex-slave plantation whose far-flung boundaries bordered on Rhoden Hall. Residents of the district will

Birthplace of a King: the house where Bob was born (above) still stands as sturdy as ever at Nine Miles, St. Ann. Below left: Bob at age 16 in Trench Town— all adorned in his 'best' Sunday suit. Below right: Bob, Rita and Peter Tosh demonstrate their unity in the late 60s, a period when Bob operated his own record shop (opposite page).

40

"During school break, de teacher she say, 'Who can talk, talk; who can make anything, make; who can sing, sing; and me sing."

(As told to Jon Bradshaw, *Newsday*, 14/8/77)

tell the visitor that Norval had served in the British Army, and was commonly referred to as "Captain".

One day, while on horseback, the captain, reportedly a vigorous man in his fifties, is said to have spotted Cedella while visiting the village, and the courtship began. The house where Bob was born no longer stands, but the site is close to the single winding roadway that passes through the village.

Little did the sleepy little hamlet know that Bob Marley would have "so much things to say," that his cries for love, peace, unity, self-

respect, dignity and cultural pride for all humanity would vibrate so effectively around the four corners of the earth, just like the cries of Marcus Garvey, Martin Luther King and other heroes of the cause.

Soon after Bob's birth, the family moved to a nearby village called Nine Miles (because of its distance from St. Ann's Bay) and it is there that Bob spent his childhood. Those early days in the lush green surroundings of the rural countryside were lived simply. The rural existence was hard; and, as Mrs. Booker recalls, things were not made any easier when the captain left St. Ann to take up another job in the city, leaving Bob's mother with the sole responsibility of raising him, on her meagre earnings. But in the hills one could find tranquillity.

> Sun is shining, the weather is sweet
> Make you want to move your dancing feet. . . .
> When the morning gather the rainbow
> Want you to know, I'm a rainbow too

> ("Sun Is Shining")

Bob spent his days among uncles, aunts and an assortment of other relatives who doted on the child of mixed parentage, "the likkle brown bwoy." He had a gift for music, and a cousin, Nehemiah Lemonious, made him his first guitar out of a large herring pan with strings attached to a wooden fretwork. Meanwhile, Bob's mother, a deeply religious woman, was always singing spirituals, and this nurtured his sound sense as a youth. Many years later he would tell her that whenever he sang, he felt the same way as she did when she sang in church and got into the spirit. Then there was Bob's grandfather, Omariah Malcolm, who taught him many things about life, and had a sound system—turntable, amplifier and large speakers—that was a musical medicine show: a good remedy for whatever ailed you.

At school, Bob took more interest in action songs than classwork. "The teacher say, 'who can write, write. Who can sing, sing.' So me sing," Bob once recalled. He was bright, but more meditative than aggressive toward learning.

For a time he lived between the country and the city.

> **I feel so high, I even touch the sky**
> **Above the falling rain**
> **I feel so good in my neighbourhood**
> **So here I come again**
>
> ("Kaya")

But he left the hills finally in his early teens, in the late fifties, when his mother decided to answer that clarion call that beckons Jamaican country people, like so many others, to gather their belongings and migrate to the city, away from the cock's crow that one morning seems too near to the ear.

So mother and son made their way to Kingston; and they stopped in Western Kingston, where so many rural migrants stopped. This periphery of the city was a depressed, low income area full of squatter settlements; dotted with government "yards" (a small group of rental apartments with communal cooking and sanitary facilities built by the colonial government). The post-Independence government eventually stopped building these, replacing them with high-rise apartment buildings which changed the character of the area, so that it became known as "Concrete Jungle".

The Concrete Jungle, where streets are paved with too many people, with dreams too big, in too little space, poised for a race which knows no fair pace.

"Who is Mr. Brown? . . .
What a thing in town
Crow chauffeur driven around
Skanking as if they have
Never known the man
They call Mr. Brown . . ."
(Mr. Brown)

CHAPTER 3

CONCRETE JUNGLE

Cold ground was my bed last night
And rock was my pillow too

("Talking Blues")

THE ABOVE more than aptly describes the physical and mental environment that served as an immediate reference to the reality of living in the Concrete Jungle. Lines of social and economic demarcation are most clearly drawn here. A place where the haves choose not to be and the have nots have no choice.

No chains around my feet but I'm not free
I know I am bound here in captivity. . . .

("Concrete Jungle")

Western Kingston. Commonly referred to as "Kingston 12", based on the postal zoning. Concrete Jungle, Trenchtown, Jones Town, Denham Town—the names of some of the different areas of the same district. Birthplace of the downtrodden and the oppressed, den of inequity, where the strengths of the mightiest are tested merely in

order to stay alive, where the weak definitely fall by the wayside. Unfortunately, for the many who remain trapped there, the situation is unchanged. Still.

In Kingston 12, the social deprivation was a far cry from the tranquillity of Nine Miles. The people lived in crumbled and ugly low cost housing. When Mrs. Booker and her son arrived, most of the area was basically one vast squatter settlement. Many shelters were makeshifts of tin, wood and cardboard scraps. It was not uncommon to find eight or more people living in a room 7 by 10 feet. Human waste was deposited in holes, in between the mountainous rubbish heaps. In Dungle, the most infamous of these areas, residents scavenged goods for building, selling, and eating in competition with the local "john crows" (Jamaican vultures). Not everybody lived in such deplorable conditions. For instance, there were the yards that the colonial government had built, where you occupied one room in a barrack, shared an outhouse and a kitchen, and did your bathing and laundry under a tap in the middle of the yard. But too few people were lucky enough to get such a home.

> **Oh I remember when we used to sit**
> **In a government yard in Trenchtown**
> **Observing the hypocrites**
> **Mingle with the good people we meet . . .**
> **Then we would cook cornmeal porridge**
> **Of which I'd share with you. . . .**
>
> ("No Woman No Cry")

In the mid-sixties, the government cleared most of those squatter settlements and constructed high-rise apartment blocks in their place. That was good. What was not good was that the grateful apartment dwellers, now diehard supporters of the government, and the others who had not been so influenced, started expressing their political differences in extreme ways. This was not too surprising. When you are a youth with no hope it is easy to turn to violence.

This morning I woke up in a curfew
Lord knows, I was a prisoner too . . .
Burning and a looting tonight
Burning all illusions tonight.

("Burnin' And Lootin' ")

Woman, hold your head and cry
'Cos your son has been shot down on the street and died

("Johnny Was")

Not everybody turned to crime or violence. Some turned to music as a way of pleading a case for survival, wailing deep into the night.

One good thing about music
When it hits you, you feel no pain. . . .

("Trenchtown Rock")

"collective security for surety"

Bob Marley was hit by many things, and music was not the only thing that could hit you in Trenchtown. There was the badman, policeman, rentman, even your friends, man. The only productive thing one could do was "breed" a woman.

Bob used to shift around a lot. He often "cotched" (bunked) with distant relatives and friends. One such shelter was provided by Thaddeus Livingston, father of Bunny Livingston, later a Wailer.

Bob passed through almost as many schools as homes. He is said to have attended Ebenezer, Wesley, St. Aloysius and Stepney schools. He finally finished at the age of fifteen, in 1960. He started learning the welding trade, at the corner of South Camp Road and Emerald Road in downtown Kingston, some two miles east of where he was living. He disliked the trade intensely. All he was interested in was music.

From reality I just can't drift
That's why I'm staying with this riff
("Easy Skanking")

At around this time, his mother emigrated to the U.S.A., leaving Bob and a baby sister, Pearl, to live with an aunt on Fifth Street in Trenchtown.

The welding trade may not have been Bob's idea of fulfillment, but it was not without its uses. There he met co-worker Desmond Dekker, who was impressed by Bob's talent and introduced him to Jimmy Cliff, who in turn connected him to Ken Khouri's Federal studio in Jamaica. There Bob got to do his first recording, which appeared on Ken Khouri's label. The song was entitled "Judge Not". Bob was still only fifteen. The public judged, but not in his favour. Undaunted, Bob tried again, and released a tune called "Terror" for which he received the royal reward of £20. He followed that effort by borrowing "One More Cup of Coffee", a previously recorded tune by Brook Benton, and this did not fare too well either. In any case, it was released only in the U.K., and Bob received no royalties.

Incidentally, co-welder Desmond Dekker, along with his Aces, would later be one of the first Jamaican recording artistes to make a significant mark on the international charts. The single "Poor Me Israelites", which paid homage to Rastafari, landed at No. 1 on the British charts, an indication of the reckoning that was to come.

Jimmy Cliff would later feature in the five star film, "The Harder They Come", a cinematic experience of the harsh realities of living in the Kingston ghetto, which continues to draw long queues wherever it is shown.

One thing about music camaraderie is that when it is there, the notes can scale very high. The rigidity of the foundations of that mutual respect and friendship often holds the key to the continuity

Two superstars u were among the f to get Bob on his ... Bob was only in 1960 when D. mond Dekker (ab right) and Jimmy Cliff (below right collaborated to g. him his first stud. session. Dekker, whose first solo h "Honour Your Mother And Fatt exploded in 196. went on to score . million-seller, "P Me Israelites", si years later. Cliff his first hit, "Hu cane Hattie", in 1962 and event. became a superst. worldwide, starr. in Jamaica's first full-length movie "The Harder Th Come", a decade later.

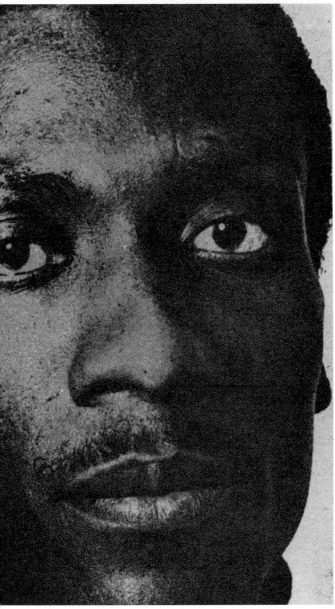

of musical expression. It also enables the musician to use humble beginnings as a more credible source of applied resolve. In the process, giving way to visions; in the end, seeing their realization.

* * *

In an interview with author Whitney, Bob's mother, Mrs. Booker, recalled early stages in the development of his career.

MLW: How supportive were you when Bob first showed signs of his musical interest?

CB: Well I was very supportive of him, in every way I could. I didn't oppose him in anything that he was doing. Sometimes he used to be out late and then when he came in I would say where you was with something in my hand to even beat him, you know. And then he used to say he was rehearsing. And then me say rehearsing what. And he said he was rehearsing some songs. But then, you know, he would go on and I never really was against him in what he was doing because you just have to stand aside and see the result of things. So I would say I supported him in every way I could.

MLW: You encouraged him to take on a trade which was welding, which he did until something happened. . . .

CB: You see, after a piece of metal get in his eye, I saw him suffer so much that night because every minute I have to run like when the light come on and he start to bawl. When he came home at first he asked me to take it out and when I take the kerchief and I do like this [*indicating motions of her hand going to his eye*] I could feel the steel and I said oh my God and I said it can't be like this and him cry the whole night through and they told him to use cold water, and a wet towel, and just rest it over the eye. So most of the night I have to do that for him, and then the morning we go to the hospital and everytime I look on him something happen to me. Something run from my toe right up . . . just a cold sympathetic feeling. I was feeling very sorry for him. Him say, "You nuh hear me say is nothing else me want to do beside sing?" And I .have to say, "Really, is true."

MLW: Some time after that you went to live in Delaware?

CB: I spent nine months [in the U.S.]. At that time Pearl [Bob's younger sister] was a baby. After I got married [in the U.S.], I went back home and I decided to get both children, Bob and Pearl, but then after I left he was still doing his [music]. He wrote me and he sent me some money. I remember it was a Saturday and me and my husband we get a little slip because when the mailman came I wasn't there so I had to go to the big post office to sign for it, and he sent the money to me and I was so happy and he told me that was money that he make. It was about two hundred dollars, he save it up in Jamaica and that was a lot of money during that time. He tell me how to save it . . . is only in them days I get letter and after him get really bigger, him telephone, him no bother with no writing again, but I could love the writing so much. I appreciate them more than a million calls. I always love to read them especially when him say, One Love, Jah Rastafari. I always just love the mood. And him say to me, when him singing him feel the same way like when I was singing in church when I go into the spirit. He used to sing some spiritual songs, him and Bunny [Wailer] together. That was very touching and me say if he say him feel like me, then he must really feel good.

MLW: What was the first performance you attended?

CB: It was in 1970 after the death of my husband, Mr. Booker. It was in Philadelphia and I went there for the first time and I'm telling you when I saw his performance, Bob didn't look like Bob to me. He looked like he was different. He was a different Bob. He wasn't the Bob that sit down and talk [with me]. On the stage up there singing, and I could see the stature of righteousness just standing up there, you know, putting forth them words, and I cry, I dance, I cry, don't know what to do, I rejoice. Me find even when them give me good seats in the front and things like that, you find everybody come before me and stand up on the chairs and me just close me eyes and let them get them desire by seeing, I don't have to for I have seen enough. I don't box nobody from me. If I can see what I am seeing, then give them the opportunity to see. And it was just a great feeling. There was a revival in my heart.

Right: Bob gives a solo performance a. the Queen's Theatr. Kingston, in the early days.

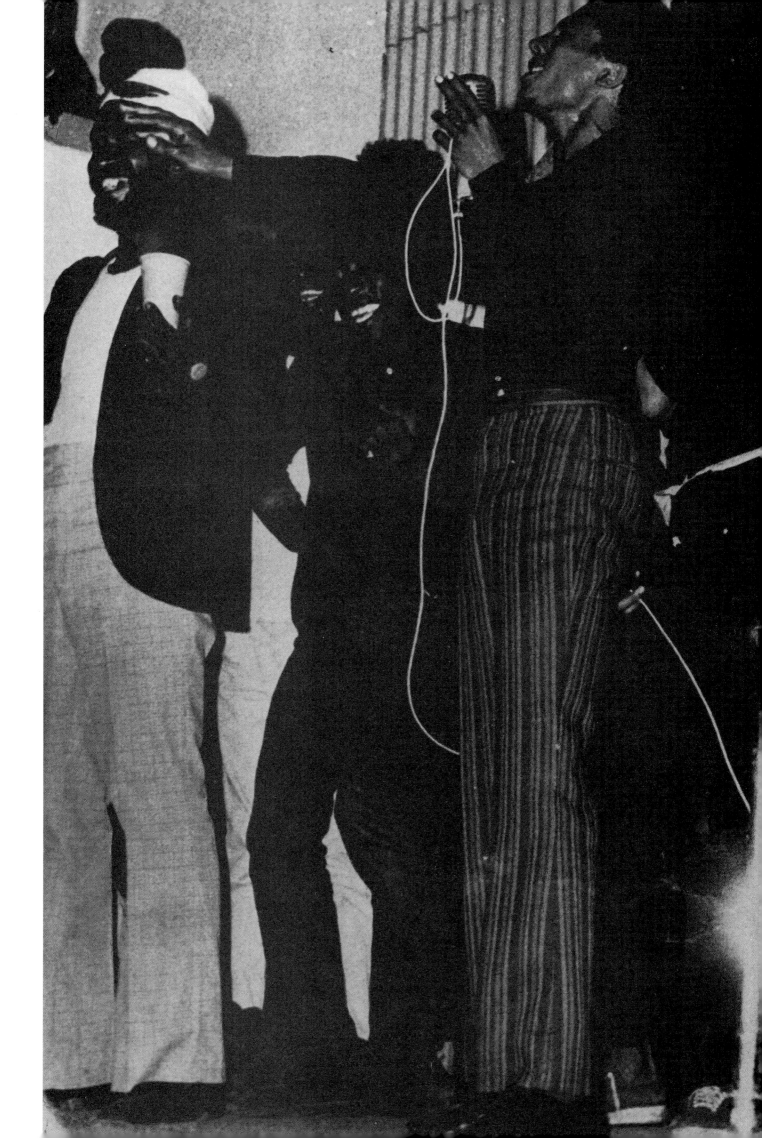

CHAPTER 4

THE WAILING WAILERS

See what we could do
Just me and you
Stir it up

("Stir It Up")

THE FORMATION of a group is usually spawned by a simple desire—to be recorded, and make a hit. Marley would later acknowledge being influenced by some of the early rhythm and blues groups like the Impressions, the Drifters, the Moonglows and others from the United States. Groups who must have shared a similar pattern of development: they would have heard their thoughts echo from the hallways and rooftops of a tenement building, while those of Marley and company probably rebounded quickly off their zinc fence abode at a volume that let their first audiences in with free general admission.

In Trenchtown, the "reggae college", Bob got together with Neville O'Riley Livingston (Bunny Wailer) and Winston Hubert McIntosh (Peter Tosh). It was 1964. Night and day, Marley, Livingston and Tosh practised and sang in the yards from First Street to Fifth Street. When Marley wasn't doing this, he was on First Street in a kitchen which was barely the size of a large box, practising into the early morning hours with a talented and close friend, Vincent "Tartar" Ford, before both passed out on the floor. As his confidence grew, Bob suggested forming a vocal group, bringing together Peter and Bunny, Junior Braithwaite and two girls, Beverly Kelso and Cherry (surname unknown). They called themselves "The Wailing Wailers".

Joe Higgs, composer and singer of the Higgs and Wilson duo, helped to form the group and gave it direction. Higgs gave lead singer Bob Marley pointers and coaching. He helped Bob to understand jazz, and would have a lasting effect on his career. Higgs also helped the group in their search for a record producer.

The time was right. In the early sixties the newborn local recording industry was beginning to draw on the music that was coming from those who existed "where the living was hardest" in Western Kingston. Talents like Desmond Dekker and Jimmy Cliff were just beginning to surface.

Clement Dodd, also known as Sir Coxsone or "Downbeat", had one of the largest rosters of Jamaican recording artists in his Studio One stable. Dodd had gained prominence through his sound system and DJs, encouraging party patrons to "lively up themselves" in a specially trademarked style.

Components of a typical sound system of the early 60s (above) which belted out the hits of the time at dance hall sessions. One of the most popular sound system operators, Clement 'Sir Coxsone' Dodd (below) later became one of Jamaica's major record producers and still operates his Studio One on Brentford Road, Kingston, where he had the distinction of producing the first hit songs by the Wailers (right) in 1964.

It was the seminal Dodd who recorded the Wailing Wailers' first single, "Simmer Down" in 1964. Released during the ska period, it was a big hit. A steady succession of hot shots, numbering more than thirty, followed, including "Put It On" (later to be re-recorded for the Wailers' *Burnin'* album), "The Ten Commandments Of Love", "Love and Affection", "Lonesome Feeling", "I'm Still Waiting", "Cry To Me", and "It Hurts To Be Alone".

Some of the recordings remained on the Jamaican charts for months at a time. Others were released in Britain, providing letters from home for Jamaican immigrants. Most of these recordings were love songs, emulating many of the rhythm and blues groups of the period, especially The Drifters. This group had a marked influence on the Wailers in the area of harmonizing.

It was around this time that Bob is known to have met Rita, his future wife. She was living in Trenchtown, and studying nursing.

She would see her favourite group, the Wailers, passing by her home every day on their way to Coxsone's, and would try to attract their attention, telling them that she could also sing and asking them to arrange something at the studio for her. They eventually organized an audition, as a result of which she was made lead singer of the group, the Soulettes. Bob managed the group, and wrote songs for them. Gradually, he developed more than a professional interest in Rita. After a time he moved in with her.

As the social conditions of the Wailers toughened, their lives and those of the youths around them hardened into a determination to survive, but by their own code of ethics. It was a personal revolution waged against the status quo. The attitude came to be described as

In the early stages Joe Higgs (right) was most instrumental in helping to form, inspire and promote the group—which was later joined by Bob's wife, Rita (top). The involvement with Johnny Nash (centre), Danny Simms and Art Jenkins led to many rehearsing sessions similar to the scene on the opposite page. From left— Peter, Bunny, Jenkins (standing with mike), Rita and Bob.

the "rude boy" culture of which the Wailers were masters. "The Wailing Rudeboys" became the group's moniker for a time when they delivered a series of songs with "rude" in the title, like "Rude Boy" and "Rudie Get Bail". Peter Tosh's "I'm The Toughest" and Marley's "Jailhouse Keep Empty" were among several other hits.

But though the Wailing Wailers had hit after hit, they were not bringing in money equal to the effort they were putting out. They were being paid only for recording sessions; in those times enforcement of royalty collections was virtually unknown and standard fees nonexistent. Sometimes a singer's compensation would be limited to bus fare and coins to hear himself on the jukebox or turntable at a dance. The tough stance characteristic of the rude boy does not seem to have been menacing enough to collect on the loose gentleman's agreement they had with Coxsone.

Unhinging from Dodd was really a matter of simple arithmetic. It was getting harder and harder to divide nothing equally.

Man to man is so unjust
You don't know who to trust
Your worst enemy could be your best friend
And your best friend your worst enemy . . . .

("Who The Cap Fit")

It was a lean period for the group. It is at this point that they became drawn by the forces of Rastafari, being inspired and motivated by certain elders in Trenchtown where they had spent most of their formative years. So it is here that the clock began its rhythmic tick - for Rastafari influences rudie and the rebel becomes a revolutionary.

They stab you in the back . . .
But Jah have them in derision
In the valley of decision

("Want More")

Both Junior Braithwaite and Beverly Kelso left the group in 1966. Braithwaite emigrated with his parents to the United States but Kelso's departure was never really explained. At the same time, Marley re-evaluated the situation and decided to head for the United States where he joined his mother who was living in Delaware, leaving Jamaica the very day after he and Rita got married. He stayed in the U.S.A. for nearly a year, holding down a few odd jobs in such places as a restaurant, a car park, and a Chrysler factory where he was able to make use of the welding skills he had acquired in Jamaica.

The sun shall not smite I by day
Nor the moon by night
And everything that I do
Shall be upfull and right
Working with a forklift
On a night shift

("Night Shift")

After losing his job Marley applied for public assistance, but received instead an unexpected invitation, an offer he chose to refuse. It was a draft notice. Not wanting to find himself in Uncle Sam's or any other trenches, he returned to Jamaica and regrouped with Bunny Livingston and Peter Tosh.

Bunny and Peter meanwhile had stretched themselves musically; during Bob's absence, Bunny had written some material and Peter had cut a few solo releases and fine tuned his guitar.

The group tried to cut it again with Dodd, but the beat missed, and Bob, Peter and Bunny decided to form their own label, "Wailing Souls". Bob marked his homecoming with a single called "This Man

is Back". Once again they produced hit after hit, popular songs such as "Bend Down Low", "Stir It Up" and "Nice Time". They opened up a record shop at Parade in downtown Kingston, which they later moved to Beeston Street. "Skill" Cole became manager for the group.

The Wailers were making waves again, but with the same result— no money. The "syndicate" that existed in Jamaica—the big producers with their large stable of artists and control of the recording facilities—was not allowing them to flourish. They were not equipped to fend for themselves nor familiar enough with the right moves to make it with the bigger guys stepping on their heels. At about this time Bunny Wailer was given a new number, not to sing but to wear, while serving a year's term in prison for smoking "ganja" (marijuana).

Marley decided that he had enough of the rat race, and retreated to St. Ann, where he tried his hand at farming. However, very shortly after, in 1968, Afro-American singer Johnny Nash and his personal manager, Danny Simms, along with Arthur Jenkins, an arranger, visited Marley in Jamaica, with the result that Marley and the group were signed to the American JAD (Johnny, Arthur and Danny) label. Nash paid for Marley to go to Europe to make an album and a film score. Only one single surfaced from the album, in the U.S.A.. The film score was never released. Nash, on the other hand. succeeded in resuscitating his musical inspiration with his cover version of the Wailers' "Stir It Up", and other Marley songs such as "Guava Jelly". These were recorded on his very successful album *I Can See Clearly Now,* for which the Wailers did the backing tracks.

Here comes the con man
Coming with his con plan . . . .

("Crazy Baldhead")

Disillusioned, Marley returned to Jamaica, and spoke of not collecting his dues for the efforts with the JAD combine. Later, during an interview, he would sum up the situation by saying: "Me don't want to say nothin' bad 'bout them, but still me no have nothin' much good to say." Nevertheless, at the end of this experience, Marley had firmly established himself as a songwriter.

Marley found the Wailing Souls label in deep trouble. In those days, administration was not the strong point of Bunny Livingston and Peter Tosh.

With time testing the bonds of their musical association, they shortened their name just to "The Wailers", without abbreviating the musical intent. If ever there was a time to project that individuality that grows out of the slow forward and fast rewind pace of trying to make it in music, it was now. All they needed was a new formula.

Enter Lee "Scratch" Perry, the producer, who remixed their ingredients until things really started to bubble. The Upsetter label was where they laid their tracks, producing wondrous waxworks that have become Jamaican music classics seemingly glued to the Jamaican Hit Parade.

Among the single hits were "Soul Rebel", "Duppy Conqueror", "400 Years", "Mr. Brown", "Small Axe", "Feel Alright", and "Come-a Come-a". The *Soul Rebel* and *Soul Revolution* albums have become treasured collector's items. The music on these two albums was some of the Wailers' finest work, supported by rhythms that are as fresh now as when they were first played. The music had a militant fervour, down to the record jacket of *Soul Revolution* depicting the Wailers on a revolutionary manoeuvre armed with guns made from wood.

Yes me friend
Them say we free again
The bars could not hold me
Force could not control me . . . .

("Duppy Conqueror")

The music did well locally in Jamaica but once again Marley, Tosh and Livingston were getting the short end. The affiliation with Perry soon soured as the personal, economic and artistic differences surfaced, and ended the way of many singer/production teams.

In 1970, the Wailers formed the Tuff Gong label. Guy Coombs, artist and one time close friend of Marley, maintained in an interview

1. SMALL AXE
2. DREAMLAND
3. CONFUSION
4. EARTHQUAKE
5. PLACE CALLED AFRICA
6. SOUL REVOLUTION
   Wailers L.P.

Upsetter RECORD SHOP 36 CHARLES STREET KINGSTON

"My name is Scratch, from the beginning, and everybody have to start from scratch. Anyone deny that, him fall. So who am I? Check it out for yourself. Don't let me tell you . . ."

(Lee "Scratch" Perry)

SWING 40

1.	No Woman No Cry	Marley and Wailers
2.	Jet Plane	Sonya Spence
3.	Send Me The Pillow	Jackie Brown
4.	Talking Blues	Cimmarons
5.	Disco Stamp	H. Bohannon
6.	So Long	Dennis Brown
7.	Legalize It	Peter Tosh
8.	The Hustle	Van McCoy
9.	Envious	Keith Poppin
10.	Pour Sugar On Me	Judy Mowatt
11.	Shaving Cream	Fabulous Five
12.	Fade Away	Junior Byles
13.	Hold On	Johnny Clarke
14.	Laughing A Little	Spinners
15.	Miss Wire Waist	Carl Malcolm
16.	Give And You'll Get	Marcia Griffiths
17.	Zion Higher	Burning Spear
18.	Zion Touch Me Baby	Tamiko Jones
19.	Pass It On	Bunny Livingston
20.	Babylon Policy	Brent Dowe
21.	Imagination	Ben E. King
22.	Reggae Got Soul	The Maytals
23.	I'm Just a Girl	Pat Davis
24.	Hooray Festival	Roman Stewart
25.	Conference Blues	Ethiopians
26.	Nyah	Bob Andy
27.	But If I	Tinga Stewart
28.	I'm So Glad You're Mine	Al Brown
29.	Peaceful Rastaman	Levi Williams
30.	Rocking Chair	Gwen McCrae

The hot

LOCAL L.P.'s

BOB MARLEY LIVE
Bob Marley and the Wailers

GARVEY'S GHOST (DUB)
Burning Spear

MOVE UP BLACKMAN
Tyrone Taylor

THE GORGON
Cornell Campbell

SING FOR I & I
Delroy Wilson

SING FOR YOU AND YOURS
Horace Andy

Memorabilia of record charts from the early 70s tell the story of the Wailers' success on the Jamaican music scene. It was with Lee "Scratch" Perry (above)—one of the most successful producers of the period—that Bob got together to write and produce such hits as "Duppy Conqueror" and "Small Axe" which were to launch the Wailers on a sound footing. Eventually Perry lost the relationship with not only Bob, but also the Barrett brothers, Carlton and Aston "Family Man" (opposite page, left and right, respectively) who were members of his "Upsetters" studio band as well as their own "Hippy Boys" band.

with Basil Walters (*Jamaica Daily News,* May 21, 1981), that the name "Tuff Gong" had been conceived when Bob and Guy were discussing the difficulties that Bob was experiencing as an independent producer. The first hitch was that radio stations refused to offer air play without the accompaniment of a label. Bob and Guy agreed that very tough times were ahead; then Guy, who shared an interest with Bob in Africa, remembered that "in Africa there is a thing called a 'gong' that gives the sound of a bell and is used for communication. So I

told him that I could design a label for him and call it 'Tuff Gong'."
From this label the name of Bob's recording studio would be born
some eight years later.

The new label was a real turning point in the Wailers' careers. For
once, the effect of scoring hit after hit made itself felt in their
pockets; and the tune "Trenchtown Rock" stands out as one of the
most memorable of these hits.

The good fortune of the new label was assured when the Barrett
brothers, Aston "Family Man" and Carlton, joined the Wailers in
1970. They came to the band with the reputation of being Jamaica's
best bassist and drummer respectively; and their double-barrel
rhythm section is still to be rivalled. Both were the Upsetters' main-
stay musicians, so "Scratch" Perry was perhaps understandably
miffed when they left. The group had by now
established for itself an excellent reputation
in Jamaica and throughout the Caribbean.
But internationally the Wailers were still
unknown.

CHAPTER 5

REGGAE CATCH A FIRE

Now the fire is burning . . .
Ride, natty, ride
Go deh dready, go deh

("Ride Natty Ride")

IN 1972, reggae broke through to international attention with the release of the film, "The Harder They Come", featuring Island Records' biggest reggae artiste, Jimmy Cliff. That same year, Chris Blackwell inked the Wailers to his own company, Island Records. Blackwell is said to have long cherished the hope of such a feat though he had been discouraged by the Wailers' reputation of being "dread" (difficult) to deal with.

Born of a wealthy family, Blackwell grew up in Jamaica. He was something of an adventurer, and started recording Jamaican popular music when he found himself with juke-boxes which he literally had to find music to fill. He formed Island Records in 1959 in Jamaica, and opened it in London as a British company in 1962. The name of the label is said to have been inspired by Alec Waugh's novel, *Island In The Sun*. Blackwell has become reggae's only successful international producer, and his entry into the music signalled reggae's move into the international scene.

Everybody benefitted in the new Wailers-Island relationship. This was quite a change for the Wailers, who were used to the Jamaican type of artiste/producer association which would invariably be musically productive, but financially unrewarding for the artiste. The Wailers were now given open access to a studio, were provided with the best recording facilities, and were given the treatment that had eluded them—and any other reggae artiste—in the past. It was the big break that most artistes hope for, a break that would telegraph the messages that the music contained.

You a go tired fe see me face
Can't get me out of the race ...
I want to disturb my neighbour
'Cause I'm feeling so right
I want to turn up my disco
Blow them to full watts tonight
In a rub-a-dub style, in a rub-a-dub style

("Bad Card")

First off the press was the album *Catch A Fire* (1973). It launched reggae into another realm. Previously reggae had sold only on singles and cheap compilation albums. *Catch A Fire* broke all the rules. The musical line-up of the Wailers: Bob—vocals, rhythm guitar; "Family Man"—bass; Carlton—drums; Peter—lead guitar, keyboards, vocals; Bunny—percussion, bass vocals; "Wire"—keyboards. Besides the Wailers, the craft of session men like Robbie Shakespeare and Tyrone Downie, and the overdubbing of some English musicians, gave the album an unmistakable identity. It had classics like the brooding and beautiful "Concrete Jungle", "Slave Driver", and Tosh's "400 Years".

Slave driver, the table is turned
Catch a fire ... you gonna get burned

("Slave Driver")

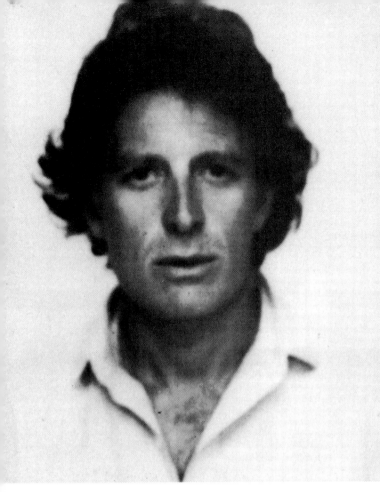

In 1972 the Wailers (top right) signed up with Island Records, owned by Chris Blackwell (top left) and became primarily an album-producing group. The following year American singer Eric Clapton (right) took "I Shot The Sheriff" from the Catch A Fire album and re-recorded it, making it the first Marley song to sell a million copies as a single.

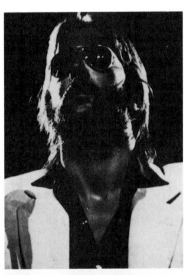

BOB MARLEY and the WAILERS.

"Dready got a job to do
And he's got to fulfill that mission
To see his hurt will be their
Greatest ambition
But we will survive
In this world of competition
Cause no matter what they do
Natty keep on coming through
And no matter what they say
Dready de deh every day . . ."
(Ride, Natty, Ride)

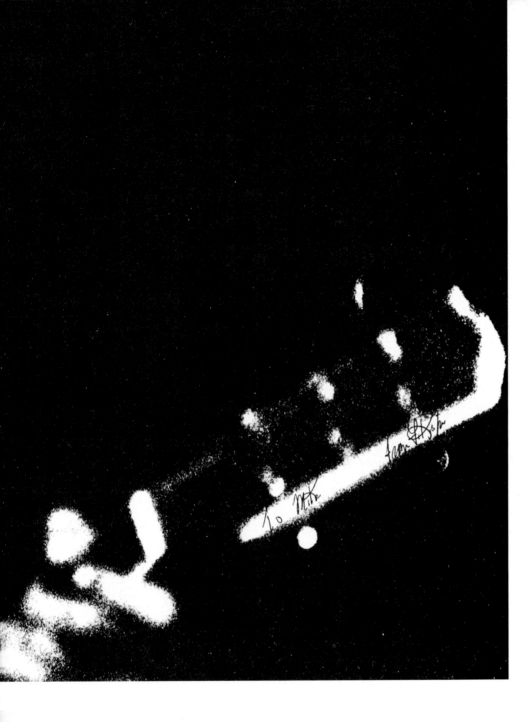

Left: Bob in performance in 1976. After Peter Tosh and Bunny Wailer left the Wailers, the group was to be comprised of people like (from left, below) Alvin "Seeco" Patterson, Earl "Wire" Lindo, Al Anderson, Junior Marvin and Tyrone Downie (conversing with Bob).

The album was acclaimed internationally, proving that reggae was a challenge to rock. The album made no impact, however, on the Jamaican public, and possibly for two reasons: too much foreign infusion of rock instruments, and the mixing out, for the international release, of the heavy "one drop" bass rhythm, which characterized real roots reggae. Indeed, the Wailers refused to release it locally until the heavy bass bottom was mixed in again.

Catch A Fire warmed the reception that *Burnin'* (1973) would receive. The sound that was in the offing was a flame which caught on like a sagebush fire. Some hot shots, like "Get Up, Stand Up", were raging; others were more subtly smouldering, like "I Shot the Sheriff"; re-recorded by Eric Clapton, it became a big chart success in America, Britain, and Germany.

> **Sheriff John Brown always hated me**
> **For what, I don't know**
> **Everytime I plant a seed**
> **He say, Kill it before it grow . . .**
> **Freedom came my way one day**
> **And I started out of town**
> **All of a sudden, I saw Sheriff John Brown**
> **Aiming to shoot me down**
> **So I shot, I shot him down**

("I Shot The Sheriff")

In the same year, the Wailers appeared with Marvin Gaye at two shows in Jamaica, one at the Carib Theatre and the other at the National Arena. At both shows they upstaged Gaye with their natural vibrations. Later in 1973, the group toured the U.S.A. with Sly and the Family Stone, who at the time were garnering chart action and live performance attention that picked up many music executives' lunch tabs. Again, the group stole Sly's thunder. The Wailers then returned to Britain to promote *Burnin'*.

But then a shift—a major one. Environmental blues, too many "pay deductions" and the need for individual expression contributed to the desire to go separate ways, and so Bunny Wailer and Peter Tosh "stepped". It was 1974.

The detachment, however, was only physical. It did not in any way weaken the important effect that their combined musicianship had had on their listening public. Both Tosh and Wailer have gone on to successful solo careers. Tosh's recordings include *Legalize It*, *Bush Doctor, Mystic Man, Wanted Dread And Alive, Equal Rights*, and *Mama Africa*. Wailer's releases include *Blackheart Man, Protest, Struggle, In I Father's House, Rock And Groove, Bunny Wailer Sings The Wailers*, and *Tribute*.

Thereafter Marley was a solo artist (with Joe Higgs helping him out for a while by standing in for Bunny). The extraordinary *Natty Dread* was released in 1975, and became the sound that dreadlocks

were grown by. Drawing heavily on the Trenchtown experience and Rude Boy/Rastafari beliefs, the album was a work of classic proportions. It had great lyrical strength, and an accompanying music that was to stamp the Wailers sound as *the* reggae sound. Particularly noteworthy were the interplay of the rhythm section of the Barrett Brothers and the blues-fed guitar obbligatos of Al Anderson, an American who had joined the group in time to complete the album. The harmony singing of the I Threes (Rita Marley, Judy Mowatt and Marcia Griffiths) replaced that of Tosh and Wailer, and gave reggae a new vocal dimension.

In the same year, Marley appeared with Stevie Wonder in Jamaica and commanded his respect. In 1975 also, the band toured Europe and recorded a live album at the Lyceum in London. *Live* and the single "No Woman No Cry" both made the charts. "No Woman No Cry" was the pick of the crop from the *Natty Dread* L.P. with its simple, understated but haunting evocation of the life of suffering that Bob had left behind but too many others were still caught in.

> **In this great future**
> **You can't forget your past**
> **So dry your tears I say . . .**
>
> ("No Woman No Cry")

Bob Marley and the Wailers had now become a force that could not be ignored. Black youth in Britain as much as in Jamaica were identifying with Rastafari, and channelling their rebellion against society into a new form of expression: dreadlocks, and tams (woolly hats) in proud red, gold and green. And white youth throughout Europe were grabbing at the first, fresh, high-energy protest music that had come their way in years.

In 1976, *Rastaman Vibration* was released, and it hit the U.S. charts. By this time, Tyrone Downie and Alvin "Seeco" Patterson had joined the band as keyboard player and percussionist respectively. For many of Marley's fans, this album would remain the clearest exposition of

"From the first I met Bob, I feel the formation of the Wailers was the idea of the Father, because the group was so spiritual. No man say mek we do this, we just sing along and man just love how it sounds . . .

"When I left the Wailers it was not directly any conflict between me and Bob. Bob was manifesting what was in him. I was at that time decorating what was inside of Bob to make it beautiful and the time had come for me to decorate what was inside of me, so I did."

—Peter Tosh

Bunny Wailer:

Unavailable for comment

"NATTY DREAD"

Children get your culture
And don't stay there and gesture
Oh the battle will be hotter
And you won't get no supper
Natty dread, natty dread now
A dreadlock Congo Bongo I
. . . Roots Natty Congo I . . .
Don't care what the world say
I and I could never go astray
Just like a bright and sunny day
Oh we're gonna have things our way . . .

his beliefs—from the aggressive resistance of "Crazy Baldhead" to the mournfulness of "Johnny Was", from the ominous unsettling message of "Who The Cap Fit" to the reverberating declaration of "War". A slightly more frivolous song, "Roots Rock Reggae", made the U.S. top ten.

> **Play I on the R and B**
> **Want all my people to see**
> **We're bubbling on the Top 100**
> **Just like a mighty dread**

("Roots Rock Reggae")

In 1976, Marley cemented his footprints on North American soil, with a very successful tour of the U.S.A. and Canada, before returning to Jamaica later that year. The island at that time was a very hot place to be in. In a small Caribbean country like Jamaica, the distance between people and politics is very short. When decisions are about to be made which affect the people, the fused end of the powder keg is reached very quickly, especially when the time comes to choose a leader.

Such was the case during the 1976 elections when then Prime Minister Michael Manley called a State of Emergency to cool the tempers which were flaring for change. There were attacks on persons and property by supporters of both main parties, the People's National Party and the Jamaica Labour Party, and others who were participating just to find a way to vent whatever frustrations they had.

It was this atmosphere that forced the government to put into effect certain controls that were designed to safeguard the citizenry of the country. Anything that was considered inflammatory, from literature to lyrics, was put under "heavy manners" (censorship). In the case of Bob Marley, several of his songs were banned from the airwaves: among them "War", "Crazy Baldheads", "Who The Cap Fit", and "Rat Race".

> **. . . when the cat's away**
> **The mice will play**
> **Political violence fill ya city . . .**
> **Rat race, rat race**
> **When you think is peace and safety**
> **A sudden destruction**
> **Collective security for surety**

("Rat Race")

Nevertheless, Marley always scoffed at efforts to associate him with one or another political "ism" (e.g. socialism, capitalism) and preferred to work instead towards uniting people. With this philosophy, he planned a free "Smile Jamaica" concert, which he said was just to show his gratitude to the people of Jamaica for the support they had shown him.

> **Get it together in Jamaica**
> **Soulful town, soulful people . . .**
> **Help them right, O Lord help us tonight**
> **Cast away the evil spell**

("Smile Jamaica")

On the afternoon before this concert, Marley and the band were practising in the rehearsal room at the old Island house at 56 Hope Road, Marley's home base, when five gunmen burst in; and the ensuing barrage of bullets caught Bob, Rita, and Bob's personal manager Don Taylor. Don apparently threw himself in front of Bob so that he was seriously wounded, but he miraculously survived. Undaunted, Marley went on to perform the concert at Heroes Circle under heavy security, and at one point during the show, exhibited his wound, to the cheers of a rather large constituency.

> **See them fighting for power**
> **But they know not the hour . . .**
> **Through political strategy**
> **They keep us hungry**
> **And when you gonna get some food**
> **Your brother got to be your enemy**
> **Ambush in the night**
> **They open fire on me**
> **Ambush in the night**
> **Protected by His Majesty**

("Ambush")

Afterwards, Marley decided that it would be wise to spend some time "cooling out" away from the island, and so went to Miami, where his mother now lived. He probably rested for a while in the Bahamas as well, where Chris Blackwell has a home.

> **No, no, no, I'm not running away**
> **I've got to protect my life**
> **And I don't want to live with no strife**
> **It is better to live on the house top**
> **Than to live in a house full of confusion**
> **So I made my decision and I left you . . .**

("Running Away")

In 1977 Blackwell introduced Junior Marvin to Bob Marley, and he became lead guitarist for the Wailers. He worked along with the others on the *Exodus* album. If there had been any doubts remaining about the band's international superstar status, they were firmly quelled with this LP. It stayed in the British charts for over a year: 56 weeks of constant jamming. Marley no longer had to be waiting in vain for the love of his international audiences, as was proved by the reception he received in his tour of Europe that year.

MAN VIBRATIO

The following year Marley released *Kaya*. Less militant and more pastoral in tone, an album predominated by love ballads, dedications to marijuana and "easy skanking", it incurred the wrath of some of the public who felt that if Marley's songs did not sound like a political manifesto, he had "gone soft". But Marley was undeterred. He understood that one of the foremost responsibilities that talent had to itself was to develop. In an interview with Stephen Davis in *Oui* Magazine, he remarked: "There comes a time when the artist can't follow the crowd. You have to be you, and make the crowd follow you."

The public was apparently reconciled; his visit to Trinidad that year was a sellout, and his tours of North America and Europe in that same year were even more successful than previous ones. The Wailers celebrated this triumph by releasing a live double album recorded during these tours: *Babylon By Bus*.

Reggae had "caught afire" and was spreading across the world. And with it was spreading Marley's message of resistance, revelation and redemption to all the oppressed peoples of the world.

the WAILERS...

(Dermott Hussey profiles those individual talents that too often remain in the recesses of public consciousness, yet combined to produce the most successful reggae band of all time: the Wailers.)

ASTON "FAMILY MAN" BARRETT, the bassist upon whose shoulders reggae rhythm rests, is a man of strong family ties. Indeed, Miles Davis, while listening to a Wailers tape some years ago in Ocho Rios, remarked, "That Family Man sure takes care of the family," meaning, if one can interpret the master, that Barrett's bass patterns hold the music together.

CARLTON BARRETT is undoubtedly one of the great reggae drummers, with an unmistakable style of sharp and cutting snare accents, the reggae drum roll, and a distinctive skipping figure on the high hat. He is especially crisp on *Uprising*.

EARL "WIRE" LINDO: his association with the Wailers began while he attended high school, when in his words he forced himself on the group. His first session was at Randy's but Wire does not recall which tune was being recorded; he does remember, however, that it was innovative for its use of two drum tracks. He played mostly piano then, but switched to electric keyboards when Herbie Hancock pointed the way. His first album was *Burnin';* he missed *Natty Dread* and *Rastaman Vibration* while working briefly with Taj Mahal. Lindo lists *Uprising* as his most satisfying album, in particular his playing on "Work". In Wire's view, the album demonstrates that Bob had a certain flair. He says, "Bob didn't really stop to try and catch up with the fads, he was really coming from a certain strength."

TYRONE "ORGAN" D DOWNIE (keyboards) was roped into the musical continuum as a schoolboy when he played with a shortlived group known as "Youth Progressives". He recorded with the group from the sixties as a session musician. In 1975 at the age of 19 he became a member of the Wailers. *Rastaman Vibration,* he muses, "was a pleasure doing . . . being the first album with the new Wailers sound, as far as the character of the music was concerned."

JUNIOR MARVIN, lead guitarist, is the most recent member of the Wailers. Born in Kingston, he left for London at an early age to study. After basic schooling, he studied music and drama while having private tuition from his father who played jazz piano, and from his uncle who played a regular J.A. sound system around London. On visiting the United States in the early seventies, he met the legendary blues guitarist "T Bone" Walker. " 'T Bone' Walker taught me a lot about blues guitar. I toured with him for about a year and did session work with Ike and Tina Turner and Billy Preston which helped to give me a varied style of playing." Marvin recorded with a variety of artists: Steve Winwood, Re-Bop, Remi Kabaka and Toots Hibbert. In 1977, Chris Blackwell introduced him to Bob Marley. "From that point on we had a great relationship and a good understanding for reggae music." Marvin has played lead guitar on five albums from *Exodus* to *Uprising* and has memorable solos on "Waiting In Vain", "The Heathen", "Sun Is Shining", the live versions on *Babylon By Bus* of "Is This Love", and "Get Up Stand Up", and others.

ALVIN "SEECO" PATTERSON, percussionist, began as a "roadie" on the *Natty Dread* album tour after Bunny Livingston's departure, before joining the band as a Wailer. A guru and "trainer" for Bob, he is credited for having introduced Bob to Coxsone at an audition at Studio One. Seeco has been an integral part of the Wailers' experience, but yet remains elusive.

AL ANDERSON, lead guitarist, was the Wailers' guitarist for a period, and in a sense still is, since his definitive solos, especially on *Natty Dread,* have become the standard by which all reggae guitar solos are judged. Working originally as a session guitarist in London, he overdubbed on *Natty Dread* and immediately became a member of the group. He played with Peter Tosh for a time but rejoined the Wailers where his best work has been recorded; for instance, as simple a thing as his lead-in on "Work" is a gem of guitar craft.

OTHERS WHO WAILED ALONG THE WAY:
KEYBOARD PLAYERS: Winston and Gladston Wright, Ian Wynter, and Bernard Harvey.
GUITARISTS: Earl Chinna Smith and Donald Kinsey.
HORNS came in first collectively on *Natty Dread,* with the Zap-Pow horn section of David Madden, Philip Madden and Glen DaCosta featuring on "So Jah Seh", before coming into full bloom on *Exodus.* Earlier, "Ska" Campbell, a baritone saxophonist, played some ska riffs between the rhythm and piano on "Road Block" and "Talking Blues", giving both a dark driving sound.

Bob (front centre) flanked by Wailers (stooping L-R) Carlton Barrett, Al Anderson, "Family Man" Barrett; (Standing L-R) Tyrone Downie, Junior Marvin, Earl "Wire" Lindo and Alvin "Seeco" Patterson.

CHAPTER 6

DREADLOCKS INNA BABYLON

Take my soul and suss me out
Check my life if I'm in doubt

("Rebel Music (3 o'clock Roadblock)")

OUT OF AN ABUNDANCE of experience Bob Marley always narrowed a very cautious eye in the direction of journalists. Few in his estimation were worthy of the credentials they carried and in trying to communicate with him, much slipped between the cup and the lip.

Fikisha Cumbo, a New York-based photographer and writer, was accorded a rare, unhurried and lengthy discussion in 1975. A patient Marley gave insights to aspects of his personality, thought, and wisdom which he had not revealed to anyone before.

*   *   *

It is Friday, 5:30 p.m., rush hour time in New York City. Bob, standing tall and proud outside his 24th floor Barbizon Hotel room, awaits my arrival. Inside are three Rastafarian friends. A television newscast is going on. Bob tells them to turn it off. Watermelon, grapes, other fruits and juice cover the table top. The tape recorder gets plugged in. Bob sits leisurely on the bed and I sit on the floor.

As the distant sounds of honking horns filter up to us, the interview begins . . .

FC: I'm interested in knowing about "So Jah Seh". Is Jah Jehovah?

BM: Yeah, Jah, Jehovah.

FC: Yeah, I thought so, you know. How does your religion affect your music?

BM: Affect? Well, religion really can't affect the music. Music is natural, you know. Me don't have a religion . . . me natural, not a religion, just a natural thing you suppose to have.

FC: How about the *I*? I noticed you use *I* a lot.

> "Bob Marley is quick, perceptive, extra sensitive. An original artiste on all counts. Singing, writing, performing, giving interviews. A self-educated, confident but suspicious man. The type of questions journalists ask him, he has reason to be. But most journalists know by now that this travelling company The Wailers is no hype. It's getting almost impossible for even the super cynics of the pop music press to find something to sneer at or crack jokes about. Nobody is laughing. Journalists know that an interview with Bob is a test for themselves. Some still don't know what their own problem is when they face Bob Marley. But they're learning."
> (Carl Gayle, "Black Music and Jazz Review")

BM: I? Because me, you, him, them, don't really mean nothin'. *[Pointing]* I, I, I, I, really mean that is the same I you know. The same *I* in *I* in *I* in *I*. That is the spirit of unity. When you use I, you know, you remove all that . . . . It is not we and them and those. Everyone is I. You can realize the same I in I is the I in that I. You know what I mean?

FC: Yeah, I'm coming from there. I thought that was where you were coming from. *[Laughter]* Yeah, that's beautiful. How did you get started in music?

BM: How? How? Like *[laughter]* like you mean how did I first [get] recorded?

FC: Yeah, like how did you get interested in singing or playing the guitar, or whatever you first started off doing?

BM: Well, I don't really know, but I know me mother was a singer first. Me mother is spiritual, like a gospel singer, right? She writes songs. I think that's where I hear her singing first, you know. And then . . . I just love music, love it, you know . . . grow with it. And so love it and do it . . . coming natural.

FC: Did you start off singing or did you start off playing an instrument first?

BM: Me start sing, then me write, then me play instrument.

FC: Talking about writing, what influences your writing? What directs your writing?

BM: Jah.

FC: Ah. Is there anything that gets in the way of that? I mean conflicts, pressures from outside.

BM: From people?

FC: People or industry or . . .

BM: Nah . . . you know, government sometimes maybe don't like what we have to say because what we have to say, too plain.

FC: Do you consider your music a gift?

BM: Gift . . . must be a gift.

FC: Why?

BM: Because, some people call everything a gift *[chuckle]*. It's a reality, you know.

The work just [comes], so you have to do it, you know what I mean. This God do all things, you know what I mean. So me personally as a man is nothin' without the inspiration of Jah. You dig it?

FC: How would you describe the kind of music you're into now?

BM: You getting a three in one music, you know. You getting a happy rhythm with a sad sound with a good vibration. You can't get a happy sound till you have a happy music with a happy vibration. It's like . . . wha' you say? What you ask me? Wha' the question is?

> **"I**t's like . . . wha' you say? What you ask me? Wha' the question is?**"**

FC: How would you describe the kind of music you're into now?

BM: How would I describe it? It's *roots* music.

FC: Why this style of music rather than another?

BM: Because it have the most . . . it have the best feelin' to me right now. It have more feelin' than any other music me hear . . . because . . . that thing, you have to feel it.

FC: Is reggae synonymous with Rastafari? I mean does it originate from the Rastafarians?

BM: Yeah! That's where reggae come from.

FC: How does the type of work you do affect your creativity?

BM: Like, I only do creative work.

FC: So it's one and the same?

BM: Yeah, pure creative work.

FC: What direction do you feel your music will go in, creatively and financially?

BM: My music? My music will go on forever. Maybe it's a fool say that, but when me know facts me can say facts, you know. My music go on forever.

FC: Why do you say that?

BM: Because it's how it feel to me. *[Laughter]*

FC: Can you name three people who influenced you musically?

BM: Who have influenced me *musically* . . . I'm a self-taught guitar player, right. Me like guitarists like Ernest Ranglin. Me like artist like Curtis Mayfield, Stevie Wonder, and James Brown. . . . Me like plenty people.

FC: Do you get together for relaxation with other musicians?

BM: How?

FC: Hang out.

BM: Me just hang out with I ownself.

FC: What about stereotyping? You know what I mean by stereotype?

BM: Stereo? Stereo-mono?

FC: No, for instance, people might say, *all* musicians do this or that. Have you been affected by that at all?

BM: Me look inside of me. Me hardly see outside, you know. Yeah, my eyes turn inside of me. Me don't care what people do or what people say, me look for the right things, you know.

> **"My** *music will go*
> *on forever . . .***"**

FC: So what people or society say doesn't matter?

BM: To me *[chuckle]* for a time now, me don't care what them say.

FC: In your opinion, has society categorized or put musicians into a little section?

BM: Maybe, but don't follow that train, you see, we come too creative for them to put we in any bracket, you know what I mean. Very creative. We been, like, doing this thing long time and some guys think we would have been done about three times ago, you know what I mean. Too creative to let them put

you in any bracket. Now you have good musicians; the people who me call good musician, is the people who relate to me, is just because we can communicate. Like him play something, where, it nice to me, like, it's a thing like me wanna play too. That mean where we all on the same wavelength and so on. Now you have a guy who's on a different wavelength and yet him suit a different type of people. You know, some music really can't go in a class or a bracket *[chuckle]*, music free and without prejudice. Music don't care.

FC: It just want to be, huh?

BM: Yeah, music just want'a be. All you have to do is make sure them things in tune. 'Cause when it don't tune, music vex. And when music vex, it don't sound good.

FC: When you say vex, what is that?

BM: *[Strums his guitar]* That means guitar not tuned. They all gone flat. It's weird, it's foolish, not pleasing to the ears. But if the tune *[demonstrating]* rung! rung! rung! You know, then it must be nice. But if something wrong, then every ear hears it.

FC: I was singing "So Jah Seh". That tune really flips me out, you know.

BM: Which one?

FC: "So Jah Seh".

BM: You American?

FC: *[Nods yes]*

BM: Yeah? *[laughter]*

FC: Why? You thought I was something else?

BM: *[Big laughter]*

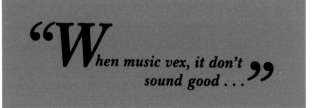

"When music vex, it don't sound good . . ."

FC: How about critics?

BM: Critics. Me no care what critics say, if me make a mistake me know me make a mistake, you know what I mean *[laughter]*. You dig it.

FC: But do they sometimes say you've made a mistake when you don't feel you've made a mistake? How about DJ's, disc jockeys?

BM: DJ great, if the music right and the people dance, DJ don't have nothing to do. Sometimes a DJ can carry a sound to the people but it have to be right, you know. I mean regardless [of] what happen, the music have to be right.

FC: I noticed when "I Shot The Sheriff" came out, I heard your tune on [the black radio station] WBLS but on the other stations I heard Eric Clapton's. Why do you think that was?

BM: Well, people don't know how to dance reggae, you know. Them don't know where the beat drop.

FC: Do you have a recording contract?

BM: I have a recording agreement.

FC: What's the difference?

BM: *[Laughter]* One is an agreement and one is a contract.

FC: Both of them have to be signed, right?

BM: Yeah, some things you agree to, some things you are contracted to *[laughter]*. Those you contracted to is those that you personally agree to, now the other one is where the guy agree to it, but because of the situation you [are obliged to] go with it. Dig it! So one is agreement and one is a contract *[laughter]*.

FC: How did you go about getting it?

BM: Well, I recorded in Jamaica, you know, and it leak out from Jamaica and go into England. And I go to England and meet up with this guy Chris Blackwell and got it together and do an album, but I find it get weird some time. . . .

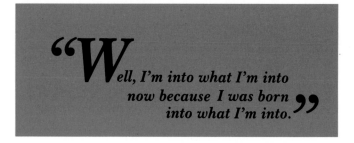

"*Well, I'm into what I'm into now because I was born into what I'm into.*"

FC: What record company are you associated with right now?

BM: Well, right now, Island have the album.

FC: Do you have a choice of your own arranger or producer?

BM: No! No! We do our own music. The guy can't really do our music. The guy don't know it, we know it.

FC:	Is it pressed and released soon afterwards?
BM:	Yeah!
FC:	I heard that *Natty Dread* was done a year ago in England?
BM:	Was it that long? No, I don't think so. About six months ago. Release date in England first, then come out in America, then Jamaica.
FC:	Why do they do it like that? Why Jamaica last?
BM:	We control it in Jamaica.
FC:	Ahh!
BM:	Because you see, we have to try to trick the guy who have the pirate mind, you know what I mean. Sometimes you release it in Jamaica, right, but you come to New York, hear the record selling here. Yet nobody have any permission to sell it here. So we have to just get a big company release it. That mean, [if a] big company catch a guy press it, [they] can destroy it, you know. Otherwise he go on and press it in him basement and keep it under cover and you still in Jamaica and never know about it. All you can do is when you come into town, you get your gun and go down there and you blast away.
FC:	*[Laughter]* Bang! Bang!
BM:	You know what I mean?
FC:	Yeah!
BM:	Good! So to skip that you deal with a big record company. Stop you from committing murder. That is how my record deal really come too, like, Island, you know. You dig it!
FC:	Are "politics" . . . when I say, "politics", I mean who you know or who knows you or who gets you into that or the other, greatly involved in your getting into what you're into now?
BM:	Well, I'm into what I'm into now because I was born into what I'm into. You dig it! You understand?
FC:	*[Nods]*

"This is what you call international music, complete music. Any music you want to play inside of reggae, you can put it here."

BM: Good! Politics! See, I'm a man of God and me come to do God's work.

FC: I'm not talking about politics in terms of the government. I'm talking about who did you know who knew Chris Blackwell in England. Was that a connection? Was it through connections that you got a thing going? Your records getting good distribution and all that.

BM: Naw, wasn't because of no connection cause we go to England; the guys who used to do them things was some big pirates, you know what I mean. So you find them guys killer of reggae music, kill rock steady and kill ska. Them guys [dracula] for reggae music, like how you have people is [dracula] for rock, you know, suck out the artist and sometime them kill him, you know what I mean. Sometimes if a guy supposed to pay an artist two million dollar, him prefer to say, "No man, I give you twenty thousand." Some big rock artist say, "So what happen to reggae music?" It's an up and down thing. It's plenty, but you understand them take so much time to come in. Like, them say they prefer something new, you know what I mean.

FC: I've seen the reggae influence in all music, from Stevie's "Boogie On Reggae Woman" to Grover Washington's "Mister Magic".

BM: Reggae music is one of the greatest musics, you know. But the only thing about reggae now is because the people in America don't really get to know how to dance it. But you see, if them can dance [to] it, then what can I tell you? You know, because *no dance* look *pretty* as reggae dance! Me know that, 'cause you can dance the whole night and it keep you in a mood. You know what I mean. You love yourself when you dance reggae music. You proud of yourself, that you come like you *born*

again! A feeling come in the music like you baptised. Yeah, you can leave from that! *[He gets up and dances]* Leave from that spiritually. Music, you know, music is great. Music can carry you to heaven, to Zion. Carry you all about to some places where you don't know. Art music, you know. Why reggae music so nice is because it's a proud music. It can be a very, very proud music.

FC: And Rastafari are very proud people.

BM: Yeah, complete. [Reggae] is what you call international music, complete music. Any music you want play inside of reggae, you can put it here. But it's the rhythm now, *that is* reggae, you know. Proud rhythm, man, them rhythm can't end. There is nothing on earth like music that can't go out. It have a different touch. Yeah, the music is a great music, man. This type of rhythm, it's earth rhythm, roots! So you find it can't go out, it's like from the beginning of time, creation. Pocomania* type of music, Rasta, the whole thing, together. And all of them people in Jamaica play it.

FC: Reggae is played all over Jamaica?

BM: Yeah, man! Now, you have blessed reggae, you know. *[Laughter]*

FC: Ahh. Tell me about that.

BM: Blessed reggae is a reggae when you try, like when you deal with reality. You get more music, more anything. You feel dirt, the earth, and you play any way, you feel it different from just thinking about it, just an imaginary thing. You know what I mean?

FC: Yeah, I really want to compliment you on the album *Natty Dread*. Yeah, it's bad. "So Jah Seh" touches something inside. I mean it's so spiritual, but you have to be in tune to it to know where it's coming from.

*Pocomania: Jamaican revivalist cult.

BM: Reggae music, man, is a raasclaat* music where you have to be proud, you have to know what creation is. When you get up in the morning, you have to be proud. You know what I mean. You have to be a sufferer who say to yourself, "Feeling all right." So you have a feeling now. So you come out and you reach for a chalice *[takes a deep breath]*. You don't wanna hear no rock music, because you can't do that right now. 'Cause rock music really calls for neon lights, plenty lights. See, a good reggae

music, now, you can be anywhere. You can be in the hills, you know what I mean.

FC: Do you feel you've obtained success in your career?

BM: Success in my career. Well, I've been always successful from beginning. No bond here, you know. An Aquarian control.

FC: What's your rising sign?

BM: Well, me never know nothing 'bout that.

*raasclaat: Jamaican expletive

FC: What's your moon sign?

BM: Me never know nothing 'bout that neither. Me just know some natural things.*[Laughter]*

FC: About your success, when you say you've always been successful, you mean inward success?

BM: Yeah. You know, me always can do what me want to do, you know. Just in time, everything happen just in time. Like you see, God is my father and him grow me just the way a son suppose to be grown. You know what I mean?

> **"*J*ah is my father and him grow me just the way a son suppose to be grown . . .**"

FC: Yeah, I know what you mean. That's beautiful. That's the truth.

BM: The perfect father for me. *[Laughter]* Just the perfect father. Everything just in time, all of those things and love, just in time.

FC: Does it help you do anything? Or does it hinder you from doing anything?

BM: Success? No, but, you see, my success is success. It's like we come with success. We don't get success, we come with it. I am success myself. That is where success is *[pointing inward . . . laughing]*. You know what I mean?

FC: Yeah. You know, it's so hard for me to keep to this format because I want to go on and talk it out. Just go on and really talk about Jah. *[Laughter]* Because that's really where it is, we're 25 years out of the Age of Aquarius.

BM: Yeah?

FC: Yeah. So we're dawning on the Age of Aquarius, which is the Age of Brotherly Love, you know, and it seems like there are so many movements in which many people are getting tuned in. Maybe that might be the force that's needed to counteract all this negativism on the earth.

BM: That's right. We need positive vibrations. 'Cause first thing you cannot be ignorant, you have to be very intelligent. You can't come tell me 'bout white and black or pink and blue, you know what I mean. We fly a colour which is red, gold and green. Now that is our colour, you know what I mean, red, gold and green. Now we're not prejudiced, because we leave our judgement unto Jah. Now maybe it's to show people who read certain things, when we grow just how we on the earth supposed to be. That is what we're dealing with. I tell you because you can't do it. You can't be two things at one time. If you positive, you have to be positive. If you negative, you have to be negative. We can't be positive to you and then negative to someone else. We can't deal with it that way. Be positive to black, pink, blue, green, yellow, everything. So me have to deal in positive. Want to cut the negative thing out entirely. Negative, outside. It's what your mouth say keep you alive. It's what your mouth say, kill you. And the greatest thing is life. So that is a thing where Jah put you through now. Weed out most of the

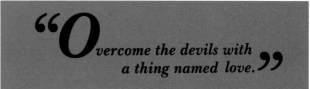

"**O**vercome the devils with a thing named love."

devils, overcome the devils with a thing named love.

FC: About the music world, are you satisfied with things as they exist now, in the whole industry situation?

BM: Me not of the world, you know *[chuckle]*. Me live in the world but I'm not of the world. Me don't care about people. Me never know who own this [hotel]. It's like Jah say, the West must perish. It's devils' country all right.

Devils are real people and capitalism and penalism [are a] type of devilism and draculazing. It's devil controlling. It's devil running part of earth, you know, while God is in Africa waiting for we to agree that there's devil running this.

FC: What effect do you feel the industry might have on musicians?

BM: You see, the whole thing is in music. Now you must realize you have guys out there, you have plenty guys who play. The only thing is, in music, man, you see, the hustling type of music, me can't deal with it. Like people who hustle music, you know what I mean?

FC: When you say hustle, what do you mean?

BM: A type of musician who go out and just sing other people's music. That mean me don't really have nothing to say for myself. Me just learn a thing me can copy then me can deal with it. Them guys suffer plenty sometimes. But, the music business man, you know, you don't question the how, because you can't know the guy who own the music. Who the guy is? You can't be caring, you know what I mean. You have to do what you have to do. Do your own thing if you want. Some people get trapped, you know.

FC: What are the types that get trapped?

BM: The men type . . . the men type.

FC: The main type?

BM: The men type, m-e-n. You have man and you have men.

FC: Tell me about that.

BM: Man is man, you know, and men is men. Now you have lots of things that men do, man don't do [chuckle].

FC: Do you feel there is going to be any change in the industry as you know it now?

BM: The only change [that] can be in the industry as we know it now is [if we make the changes happen]. The people who do the music. The people who have the music, because they have to protect them ownselves. Because, other people just hustlers. Now you can't have a guy who own record studios and yet him don't know "G" [musical note]. You know what I mean. Yet him want capitalize off music so much. You dig it? So, it's the people who do the music. It's them should control the thing. Them guys that run it is not able to control it.

FC: Are you involved in any group effort to control your own artistic creations?

BM: Yeah, I have a group named Tuff Gong. It's our company in Jamaica.

FC: Are you involved with Danny Simms and Johnny Nash in some kind of business situation?

BM: Yeah, them guys . . . me know [them] long time in Jamaica and we come together, you know. We still have a publishing agreement with them.

FC: Are there musicians whom you know that should be more well known?

BM: You have plenty musicians who should have been more well known. Now you have man like Roland Alphonso, you have Johnny Moore, man like Ernest Ranglin. Them guys there is top musicians.

FC: What do you feel about the economic situation of black musicians?

BM: What it is, man, is that we get a raw deal from people and even sometimes it is the black guy [ripping us off] because him don't really get ahead. If your mind don't sharp . . . because dig this, the thing don't just happen in the air . . . it happen in reality. One day you start think about . . . *the business*, and see all them big guys sit on all them desk [there]. Just parked out the parkin' lot like a car. Pure big guys control the record business. You know what I mean? You must get rip off. So the business go. The only way you don't get rip off is when you don't do it. But you see, once you start, you get rip off. The only one who don't get rip off is the one who don't start *[laughter]*. I tell you that. It's like me say, people know good music, you know. You can't have a good sound and let the music go all over. Hey! You know how plenty music get lost? In mixing. You know what I mean. You can't rate music with popularity. You have a guy who can play so much good music and him don't even go in the studio. Good music is the thing, any good music. Now, what good music mean is you can have fast good music and slow good music. But you know, medium music is what me call good music, everyone can move to, like reggae.

FC: How long have you been working professionally?

BM: How you mean professionally?

FC: Getting paid for it.

BM: Now, we always get rip off, you know what I mean, but we still was professional *[laughter]*.

FC: What does Rasta mean?

BM: Righteousness.

FC: *[Pause]* Okay, that's it. Thank you Bob, that was beautiful. "So Jah Seh."

BM: Irie, thanks.

FC: Yeah.

BM: Rastafari!

(Edited with permission from interview with Fikisha Cumbo dated 20th June 1975)

CHAPTER 7

IN PRAISE OF A PROPHET

Oh children weep no more
Oh my sycamore tree, saw the freedom
   tree
Oh children weep no more
Weep no more, children weep no
   more

("Time Will Tell")

MARCUS MOSIAH GARVEY is the legendary twentieth century prophet whose philosophies affected Bob Marley profoundly—directly through Garveyism or indirectly through Rastafari. Garvey is today considered to be one of the apostles of black liberation, whose theories of social reform provided some answers to the plight of the so-called disenfranchised. He is one of Jamaica's National Heroes, and his teachings are learnt and revered by every Jamaican school child. This was not the case during his lifetime, however, when—especially in his homeland—he was regarded as being nothing more than a con man.

> **They got so much things to say . . .**
> **But I'll never forget, no way**
> **They crucified Jesus Christ**
> **I'll never forget, no way**
> **They sold Marcus Garvey for rice . . .**
> **So don't you forget no way**
> **Who you are, where you stand in the struggle**

("So Much Things To Say")

Garvey was born on August 17, 1887, in the parish of St. Ann. As he matured, he became increasingly aware of racial discrimination. He embarked on an extended pilgrimage through the West Indies, South and Central America, and much of Western Europe, and was unable to find any place to which the black man could truly belong, with which he could fully identify. "I asked: 'Where is the Black man's government? Where is his King and Kingdom?'."[1] Such an empire had existed many centuries before in Africa, though white historians tried to obscure such a fact, and Garvey came to believe that it could be re-created.

> I have a vision of the future and I see before me a picture of a redeemed Africa, with her dotted cities, with her beautiful civilization, with her millions of happy children going to and fro. Why should I lose hope, why should I give up, and take a back place in this age of progress?[2]

Garvey returned to Jamaica, and in 1914 founded the Universal Negro Improvement Association, whose motto was "One God, One Aim, One Destiny." In 1916 he set up the first branch of the UNIA in the United States, and by 1919 the Association had a membership of two million.

Garvey emphasized the idea of Africa for Africans at home and abroad. This was a revolutionary idea at a time when only two African nations were independent. His Back to Africa Movement inspired a sense of identity, purpose and pride in a people so demoralized by slavery that they had long ago forgotten what such words meant. Garvey's teachings focussed on the unification of all black people, and stressed the necessity of economic and cultural development. He spoke out ceaselessly against injustice and inequality throughout his travels. He fought against the so-called leaders of his race who told the black man that a better day was coming in Paradise. This may be so, Garvey declared, but: "We also realize that we are living on earth, and that the things that are practised in

Paradise are not practised here . . . [so] we shall occupy a firm position; that position shall be an emancipated race and a free nation of our own."[3]

> **Most people think**
> **Great God will come from the sky**
> **Take away everything**
> **And make everybody feel high**
> **But if you know what life is worth**
> **You'll look for yours on earth**
> **And now you see the light**
> **You stand up for your rights**

("Get Up Stand Up")

Garvey devised a plan to realize his most important dream, that being the repatriation of the black man to Africa. He did succeed in establishing a shipping line—the Black Star Line—and in negotiating the acquisition of a land agreement in Liberia (West Africa), but his efforts were thwarted when he was charged with fraud and income tax evasion by the American government in 1922, and subsequently deported. As with most exponents of radical change, the powers that be had employed full-time extinguishers to put out the fires of hope that Garvey's platform offered. For instance, Garvey had earlier had to defend himself from the allegation that the UNIA sought to aggravate racial discord:

> We are organized, not to hate other men, but to lift ourselves, and to demand respect of all humanity. We have a programme that we believe to be righteous . . . we declare to the world that Africa must be free, that the entire negro race must be emancipated from industrial bondage, peonage and serfdom; we make no compromise, we make no apology in this our declaration.[1]

Undaunted, Garvey returned to Jamaica, where the masses greeted him as a hero and the elite scorned him. Thereafter, he tirelessly continued his preaching, moving mainly between the West Indies and the U.K. He died in London in 1940. It took some 25 years before Jamaica officially acknowledged his influence on the black destiny and declared him a National Hero. At this time his body was brought home to Jamaica, and re-interred at National Heroes Park.

> **Guiltiness shall rest on their conscience . . .**
> **These are the big fish**
> **Who always try to beat down the small fish**
> **They would do anything**
> **To materialize their every wish . . .**
> **Woe to the downpressor**
> **They'll eat the bread of sad tomorrow . . .**

("Guiltiness")

Garvey will long be remembered for the proclamation: "Look to Africa, where a Black King shall be crowned, for the day of deliverance is near." As if in answer to this prophecy on November 2, 1930, Ras Tafari ascended the Ethiopian throne and took the name Haile Selassie, which means "Power of the Trinity". He was the ruler of a monarchy that was thousands of years old, that claimed descent from Solomon, Son of David, King of the Jews, in a line of 225 centuries of Kings with the inherited title: King of Kings, Lord of Lords, Conquering Lion of the Tribe of Judah.

In Jamaica, some religious enthusiasts connected this news to Garvey's proclamation. They studied their Bibles, and found confirmation that His Imperial Majesty was the true Messiah in the second coming. A new religion was born. His Imperial Majesty became the Godhead for numerous Rastafarians, who recognized that blacks were the true children of Israel, the chosen people. Thus Garvey is regarded by many as a prophet, the John the Baptist, of the Rastafari movement. In fact, without him there may well have been no Rastafari.

> As one who knows the people well, I make no apology for prophesying that there will soon be a turning point in the history of the West Indies and that the people who inhabit that portion of the Western Hemisphere will be the instruments of uniting a scattered race who before the close of many centuries will find an Empire on which the sun shall shine as ceaseless as it shines on the Empire of the North today.[5]

"In the beginning was the Word, and the Word was with God, and the Word was God. The same was in the beginning with God. All things were made by him; and without him was not any thing made that was made. In him was life; and the life was the light of men. And the light shineth in darkness; and the darkness comprehended it not."

(*St. John 1; 1-5*)

*Jah live,
Children—yea
ah-Jah live,
Children—yea*

The new surge of interest in Garvey's beliefs in the mid-sixties in Jamaica coincided with the birth of a new social and spiritual awareness in Bob Marley as he began to question the deprivation and inequalities that he saw around him, in Western Kingston and the world, and as he began to explore Rastafari. As he matured, he related more and more closely to Garvey's teachings, and reflected them in his own philosophies.

> **We're the generation**
> **Who trod through great tribulation . . .**
> **We know where we're going**
> **We know where we're from**
> **We're leaving Babylon**
> **Into our Father's land . . .**
> **Jah come to break down downpression, rule equality**
> **Wipe away transgression**
> **And set the captives free**
> **Exodus, movement of Jah people**

("Exodus")

Marley extended Garvey's belief in the salvation of the black race to include all the oppressed peoples of the world. He called for brotherly love between Jah's children.

> **So Jah seh**
> **Not one of my seeds**
> **Shall sit in the sidewalks**
> **And beg bread . . .**
> **Puss and dog to get together**
> **What's wrong with loving one another . . .**
> **And down here in the ghetto**
> **And down here we suffer**
> **But I and I hang on in there**
> **I and I, I nah let go . . .**

("So Jah Seh")

Marley's songs became a cry for revolution.

> **It takes a revolution**
> **To make a solution . . .**

("Revolution")

In his more militant moods he could sound threatening to the status quo. A hungry mob is an angry mob, he warned. His lyrics could have a violent edge, foretelling of burning and looting, burning all pollution, all illusion.

> **If you are a big tree**
> **We are the small axe**
> **Sharpened to cut you down**
> **Ready to cut you down**
> **These are the words of my master**
> **Know that we shall prosper**

("Small Axe")

But ultimately Marley's call was not for violence but for a firm moral stand against oppression.

**I and I no come to fight flesh and blood
But spiritual wickedness in high and low places
So while they fight we down
Stand firm and give Jah thanks and praises**

("So Much Things To Say")

He never lost sight of Garvey's vision of hope, of a Zion here on earth.

One basic similarity between Marley and Garvey is the seemingly endless reservoir of energy which they both directed towards the good of the people. They both spoke of the individual who was wrapped up in his own small space and could not see the world of mankind of which he was a part. Both the literate and the illiterate listened to their urgings and pleas for the betterment of mankind. Both Garvey and Marley rallied around a flag that, when it waved in the wind, was an immediate source of identification, and telegraphed for untold miles the message that black people do have a tremendous stake in themselves.

Garvey's words were a credo, and the uttering of them was a rehearsal for what was inevitably to come, a serious battle for personal freedom.

No one knows when the hour of Africa's redemption cometh. It is in the wind. It is coming one day like a storm. It will be here. When that day comes, all Africa will stand together, 400 million strong.[6]

Marley spread the news of that battle across the world from east to west, inspiring and extending Garvey's vision of a new day.

1 Amy Jacques Garvey, *Garvey and Garveyism* (New York, and London: Collier Press, 1970), p. x.
2 ibid., p. 128
3 ibid., p. 127
4 ibid., p. 125
5 ibid., p. 9
6 ibid., p. 128

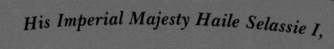

His Imperial Majesty Haile Selassie I,

King of Kings, Lord of Lords, Conquering
Lion of the Tribe of Judah.

CHAPTER 8

SO JAH SEH

Lord knows how I get from the heartaches
Lord that leadeth me yeah!
And now I'm by the still water

("Cry To Me")

WITHOUT doubt, the single most crucial cultural contribution of the Rastafarians has been music. Jamaica's special syncopated sound, the off-beat one-drop beat of roots-rock-reggae, is now being acclaimed as the music of the 1980s. Reggae is a fundamental fusion of mento, calypso, soul, rhythm and blues and jazz interwoven and superimposed on the rock-steady bass beat. The musicians responsible for developing this impelling sound are primarily Rastas. And the searing social commentary and spiritually inspiring lyrics contained in the island's mystic message music make reggae internationally relevant. Thus it is correct to state that the roots of reggae are dub-rockers (Jamaican style) and the roots of rockers are the message and drum-beat (the words, sound and power) of Rastafari.

The work of Bob Marley, a devout Rastafarian, represents all the best of this musical form. Marley's music led the way in gaining international recognition for reggae, which, incidentally, is Latin for "to the King". True reggae music is in praise of Jah.

> **Doing it, doing it, doing your thing**
> **Give Jah all the thanks and praises . . .**
> **Live it up, live it up, live it up, live it up**
> **Give Jah all the thanks and praises . . .**

("Crisis")

The Rastafari movement was born in Jamaica in 1930 when news of the crowning of Ras Tafari (Haile Selassie) as King of Ethiopia attracted the attention of various Jamaicans who had been to some extent influenced by Marcus Garvey. They connected Garvey's prophecies of the crowning of a black king who would deliver black people from their oppressors, with certain biblical passages that confirmed to them that Selassie was indeed the Messiah. Interestingly, these persons are said to have reached this conclusion quite independently of each other.

Among the key figures in this birth were Leonard P. Howell, Joseph Nathaniel Hibbert, H. Archibald Dunkley and Robert Hinds. All were ministers, who formed separate groups based on this revelation.

Howell is the man most credited with the initial spreading of the Rastafari way of life. He was a well-travelled man and was reported to have fought on African soil and to have command of an African language. Howell had stationed himself for a period of time in North America where the social ravages of racism were common practice. This directed his intent in working for necessary reforms. He began his ministry in the slums of Western Kingston.

RAS TAFARI

Hibbert was a member of the Ancient Mystic Order of Ethiopia, a secret society, who after spending many years in Panama returned to Jamaica and began preaching of Emperor Haile Selassie as the returned Messiah. Hinds was his deputy. Hibbert started his mission in St. Andrew, and came to Kingston to find Howell preaching the same doctrine.

Dunkley, a Jamaican seaman, studied the Bible independently for over two years and concluded that Haile Selassie was indeed the Messiah that Marcus Garvey had prophesied. He started his mission in Port Antonio but soon moved to Kingston. There were several others, such as Paul Erlington, Vernal Davis, and Ferdinand Ricketts, who preached the truth as they perceived it, and the movement continued to flourish and gain momentum. By 1934 a solid nucleus of Rastafari had been established in Kingston.

> "Jah live, children, yeah
> Jah Jah live, children, yeah
> Jah live, children, yeah
> Jah Jah live, children, yeah
> The truth is an offence but not a sin
> Is he who laughs last, children
> Is he who wins
> It's a foolish dog bark at the flying bird
> One sheep must learn, children
> To respect the shepherd
> Fools say in their hearts
> Rasta your God is dead
> But I and I know Jah Jah
> Dread it shall be dreader, dread
> Let Jah arise
> Now that the enemies are scattered
> Let Jah arise
> The enemies are scattered."
>
> **(Jah Live)**

Howell and Dunkley, in trumpeting the cause of Rastafari, both paid penance. They were jailed and became the targets of repeated harrassment, with Dunkley also being committed to an asylum. But these encroachments on personal freedom only ignited the ideologies and practical solutions that Garvey had to offer and Bob Marley had the yearning to embrace.

> **So Jah seh . . .**
> **Fear not the mighty, dread,**
> **'Cos I'll be there by your side**
>
> ("So Jah Seh")

One of the forefront figures in the fourth decade of Rastafari is Mortimer Planno. Planno has been attributed with being a major influence in Bob Marley's embracement of Rastafari, which occurred in his late teens. Planno is an articulate and educated Rasta elder who has been one of the movement's main spokesmen, serving as a communicator and liaison between the establishment and some of the Rastafarian community, particularly in the sixties. He became well known outside the Rasta community when he greeted Haile Selassie on his arrival to the island in April 1966. Planno, along with other elders, frequently visited Western Kingston, and it is there that Marley is said to have encountered him.

In a television interview with Gil Noble on WABC-TV (a station in New York City) in November 1980, Marley spoke of his devotion to Rastafari:

GN: A lot of people are confused about what a Rasta really is and have a very negative image of Rasta. Tell us what a Rasta is.

BM: See, Christ promised that he will return within 2,000 years. And so when Him come, he will be the King of Kings, the Lords of Lords, the Conquering Lion of The Tribe of Judah. Through the lineage of King Solomon and King David. Now my life have great meaning to me. So I really search to find out if God is here. And I search and I look. I look in Ethiopia. I look all about. I look in Germany because I'm not prejudiced. I look for God. I look in Ethiopia and I see one man stand up with these names, Emperor Haile Selassie, name King of Kings, Lord of Lords, Conquering Lion of the Tribe of Judah, through the lineage of King Solomon and King David written in the Bible. One of my things is that . . . they say that King James edit the Bible. Now my understanding is that if King James edit the Bible, I don't think he would edit it for the benefit of black people. So when the revelation turn out that Haile Selassie is the King of Kings and the Lord of Lords, straight through the lineage of King Solomon and King David, then you really know that this is the Christ return. Because we know in this world that when the white man edit it, he wouldn't edit it in our behalf. He would more edit it to make it look like England would be the big thing. But in the last days, it prove that it's Ethiopia, Haile Selassie, you know, and Haile Selassie name is Rasta. So we are called Rasta, called by his name.

True Rastafarians are rarely questioned with genuine honesty regarding the knowledge which they hold so sacred. The most devoted members try to avoid the casual scrutiny to which they are generally subjected. When possible they seek refuge away from the polluted cities in preference to higher heights—both mental and physical. They do not wish to be at the other end of the cordless mike of the curious.

How does one then define "Rastafarianism"? It is difficult, firstly because Rastas do not acknowledge this word. The correct word is "Rastafari" (pronounced Rasta-far-I). "Rastafarianism", like any "ism", has, to Rastas, connotations of temporariness, of superficiality, of being considered as just another movement due no more respect than any other "ism", such as "capitalism" or "communism". An "ism" is easy to take lightly. An "ism" is open to skepticism. "Rastafari", on the other hand, embodies a totality that cannot be qualified. It is positive. It suggests permanence, profundity, an entire way of life. One believes in an "ism". With Rastafari, one *knows*. The word "belief" is not in the Rasta vocabulary.

Rastas know that Haile Selassie, Emperor of Ethiopia, is the Messiah. This knowledge, Rastas hold, is accessible to all people, though few arrive at it. Everyone, regardless of race, is a Rasta deep

Mortimer Planno appeals for calm amidst the tumultuous greeting from the thousands who crammed the Palisadoes Airport (above) to welcome His Imperial Majesty, Emperor Haile Selassie 1 of Ethiopia as he alighted from the aircraft (top, left) to pay a formal state visit to Jamaica in 1966. People from all over the country, such as the Rasta and his son who wait outside the airport terminal for their glimpse at the Emperor (centre, right), accorded to H.I.M. one of the greatest welcomes ever made to a visiting head of state. Top right: taking the salute alongside Jamaica's then Governor General, Sir Clifford Campbell. He was usually accompanied by his pet dog—Lulu.

within; it is up to the person to recognize this. Therefore one does not turn Rasta, Rastafari turns one. One does not become Rasta. One becomes conscious of Rasta. Rastafari is becoming.

His Imperial Majesty is Jah (the Rasta word for God) who appeared in the flesh for the redemption of all blacks exiled in the world of white oppressors. "Jah" is an abbreviation of the Biblical "Jehovah"; Rastas cite Psalm 68:4 as a specific instruction for use of his name: "Sing unto God, sing praises unto his name: extol him that rideth upon the heavens by his name JAH, and rejoice before him."

Haile Selassie is known to be Jah because of direct descendancy from Solomon and David, and because of his inherited title, King of Kings, Lord of Lords, Conquering Lion of the Tribe of Judah, which identifies him as the living Jah whose coming was foretold in the Bible.

> And John said, "And I saw a strong angel proclaiming with a loud voice, 'who is worthy to open the book, and to loose the seals thereof?' And no man in heaven, nor in earth neither under the earth, was able to open the book . . . And one of his elders saith unto me: 'Weep not: behold, the Lion of the Tribe of Judah, the root of David, hath prevailed to open the book, and loose the seven seals thereof.'
>
> *(Revelation 5:2-5)*

Again, in *Revelation* 19:16—"And he hath on his vesture and on his thigh a name written, KING OF KINGS AND LORD OF LORDS." And in *Revelation* 22:16—"The Lord said unto St. John the Divine: I am the root and the offspring of David and the bright morning star."

The name "Ras Tafari" means "head creator" in Amharic. "Ras" is a title given to Ethiopian royalty. Rastas know that Ras Tafari is the living Jah, that Ras Tafari is not dead. Rastafarians hold that newspaper reports of Selassie's alleged death in 1975 are merely Western propaganda designed to subvert the truth. This is what Marley meant when, on October 4, 1975, in Jamaica's National Stadium where he was performing along with Stevie Wonder, he declared:

"And upon her f[o]rehead was a nam[e] written, MYSTE[RY] BABYLON THE GREAT, THE MOTHER OF H[AR]LOTS AND ABOMINATION[S] OF THE EART[H]
(Revelation [)]

> Jah live, children, yeah!
> Jah-Jah live, children, yeah . . .
> The truth is an offence
> But not a sin
> Is he who laughs last, children
> Is he who wins . . .
> Fools say in their hearts
> "Rasta, your God is dead"
> But I and I know that Jah Jah dread
> It shall be dreader dread
>
> ("Jah Live")

Ethiopia is viewed by many Rastas as the Promised Land, Zion, where black people will be repatriated, in an exodus from the Western countries where they have been in exile. It is Ras Tafari who will determine the date of this repatriation. For some Rastas, the name "Ethiopia" refers to all of Africa (as in fact it did originally). Some Rastas see Zion not so much as a physical place but as a state of being, a living reality which one perpetually heads towards, but few reach. Only the proper passages in life can lead you there.

When my work is over I will fly away home
Fly away home to Zion . . .

("Rastaman Chant")

"Babylon" is an evil force, be it a place, person or persons, or way of life. Babylon is anti-progressive, its mission apparently being to make life uncomfortable for righteous, peace-loving man. England, for instance, can be referred to as "Babylon". The police are Babylon. Western culture is Babylon. Politics, or "politricks", is a part of Babylon. Babylon is the place to beat a hasty retreat out of.

Political violence fill ya city . . .
Don't involve Rasta in your say say
Rasta don't work for no CIA

("Rat Race")

Even those who are somewhat skeptical towards Rastafari will acknowledge that Rastafari is a response to the Western mold of ethnocentricity which has chosen to obscure certain historical facts in

ow: Bob (centre)
ked by (l-r): Fitz
tley, Gil Noble,
nd's Lister He-
n Lowe and
mbe Braithwaite.

Gil: *How do you handle fame?*
Bob: *I handle fame by not being famous.*
Gil: *Come on, you know you're famous, man.*
Bob: *No, I mean you know, not to me.*
Gil: *No?*
Bob: *Not famous to me. (Laughter)*
Gil: *Some people get drunk off of fame.*
Bob: *See, I learned. I learned from I was coming in, from I just start the music. People have warned me. They show me—hey, this game is a game where if your mind don't sharp, you will lose your consciousness. So the only way you can lose consciousness is because if you figure say you are reh reh reh . . . people say you head might swell.*
Gil: *Right.*
Bob: *And if your head swell, that's it. So I just keep my head in a bandage that it cannot swell.*

an effort to demoralize the black man. For instance, too few people in the West, whether white or black, are aware that ancient Africa is confirmed to have had a glorious and advanced civilization when Europeans were cave dwellers; that ancient Egypt was inhabited by the same tribe as ancient Ethiopia—a black tribe, documented by the ancient Greeks as having black skin and woolly hair (certain European scholars would later argue that black skin and woolly hair were not sufficient characteristics to identify a race as being black). Leonard Barrett, in his book *The Rastafarians,* sums up the situation: "One can . . . conclude that Blacks, contrary to the attempts of Western writers to deny the evidence, were the founders of one of the greatest civilizations history has recorded."*

Don't forget your history
Know your destiny
In the abundance of water
The fool is thirsty

("Rat Race")

Rastafari is a challenge to Eurocentric values and a highly motivated thrust that seeks within its members its own cultural identity. The eye of the storm of Rastafari is focussed on the inherent right of a people who have long been "downpressed", to reposition themselves to their predestined and chosen place in order to function freely within the realms of the laws set by JAH.

Count Ossie—Mystic Revelat of Rastafari. "Caribbean—carried beyond shores."

Within Rastafari there are a few differences in terms of practice, but all uphold His Imperial Majesty Emperor Haile Selassie as the returned Messiah. It should be pointed out that while the fountain flows with many streams of water it does not change the substance of the matter that spurts forward. Thus whether one be of The Divine Theocracy Order of Nyabinghi, The Twelve Tribes of Israel, Ethiopia African International Congress, Ethiopian World Federation, Rastafari Movement Association, Judah Coptic or The Ethiopian Orthodox Church, through the spirit of love and reality, there is a oneness in recognition of one Jah.

We've all got to sing the same song

("Israel Vibration")

Rastafari is not dreadlocks and a spliff. It is a way of life that is not dependent on feigned social freedoms. Rastafari prefers to opt instead for something less material and more meaningful—truths and rights. In other words being in the world but not of it.

To arrive at a clear and realistic view of Rastafari, one has to see it for what it is—*a way of life.* Not a myth, cult, sect or figment of any one individual's imagination. Rastafari is the adherence to basic life principles and the expression of them through positive means.

*Leonard E. Barrett, *The Rastafarians: The Dreadlocks of Jamaica* (London: Sangsters/Heinemann Educational Books, 1977), p. 72.

Socialization within the prescribed norms of the general populace has not been the aim of Rastafari. Thus, what has developed from Rastafari's concerted effort to change is a more definitive and heightened cultural awareness through language, mode of dress, natural eating habits and the seeking of a clear channel away from the confines of captivity.

Let righteousness cover the earth
Like a water cover the sea . . .

("Revolution")

The Rastafari way of life has taken up where the dread middle passage voyage sought to disconnect. The uncut, uncombed growth of hair, or "dreadlocks" as it is commonly referred to, is the crowning antenna that keeps Rastafari in tune. Sharp perceptions and warnings of predatory dangers are the benefits. There are many who through circumstances or choice do not wear the covenant, but are nonetheless principled. Of course there are also many in disguise who are masquerading charlatans and utilize that appearance to do other than good deeds. Dreadlocks are traceable to early civilizations of Africa such as the Masai Warriors and other indigenous tribes.

"Locks" are not plaited, waxed or mixed with cow dung as many a misinformed rumour has spread. Nor are they the habitations of the creeping creature known as the "forty leg" or centipede.

The Rastafari way of speaking or "reasoning" is not illiteracy as some would have you believe, but the tailoring of the European language for more identifiable self-expression and modification of it to highlight the positive. Changes in vocabulary and syntax are also a conscious act of protest against the established mores of "Babylon".

One refers to oneself as "I and I" to express the divinity of the God that is ever present and within the individual. "I" is an assertion of individuality and of the importance of Jah. "I" is substituted for all other pronouns, such as "me", "you", "we", "them", which are considered to be too detached. Because "I" is so important, the first syllables of certain words are replaced by this sound; so that "vital" becomes "Ital," "ever" becomes "Iver", "Ethiopia" becomes "Ithiopia", "creation" becomes "Iration", for example.

> **Verily, I say unto the I**
> **I and I . . . will love I-manity**
>
> ("So Jah Seh")

The word "dread" largely associated with Rastafari (though many take exception to it) is a multi-faceted descriptive word that covers a variety of functions. It serves as an expletive, a personal pronoun, a verb, an adjective, an exclamation and a salutation. The word sums and totals the plight of the scattered ones who have found solace and comfort and become part of its numbers; those who have found a way "in" as opposed to "out" through Rastafari.

Dietary habits vary but most abhor the intake of animal products and meals are similar to those of a vegetarian.

Herb (marijuana or "ganja") is used by some as a sacrament and as a promoter of a calm and conscious temporal spirit. Some Rastafarians extol its meritorious use as food for thought. The desire to control it for capitalistic purposes has resulted in the continuous fight to keep it illegal.

> There went up a smoke out of his nostrils and fire out of his mouth . . .
>
> (*Psalms* 18:8)

If you smoke collie (ganja) you will have a common consciousness. If you have a common consciousness, it will be easier to deal with the forces that impede progress.

> **Tell you what, herb for my wine**
> **Honey for my strong drink**
> **Herb for my wine, honey for my strong drink**
>
> ("Easy Skanking")

Dress codes usually emphasize a prominence of the identity colors: red for the blood shed for the people, gold for the wealth of the people, and green for the fertility of the earth. Rastas wear loose comfortable clothing that allows for freedom of movement and circulation of air. For females, modest attire is the order.

Rastafarians do not believe in birth control, which is unnatural and against the wishes of Jah:

> Be fruitful and multiply; a nation and a company of nations shall be of thee, and kings shall come out of thy loins.
>
> (*Genesis* 35:11)

116

While Rastafari continues to generate debate, its numbers are ever increasing. What more is left for foes of Rastafari to do but stand aside and marvel at the sight of those who have endured innumerable indignities as they step progressively toward Zion. It seems to be in the interest of "men" manipulators (those of cowardly persuasion as Marley inferred) to keep the righteous ignorant of who they are and to brainwash them to deny all existence of their originality. But Rastafarian "bredren" and "sistren" remain fastened to that which claims and not disowns them.

As a clear indication of firm resolve and intensity of purpose that would seek to benefit all of mankind, Marley took the anthem-quality speech delivered by H.I.M. Haile Selassie in California in 1968, and at 33 revolutions per minute rendered a monumental peace prize offering.

What life has taught me
I would like to share with
Those who want to learn . . .

"Until the philosophy which holds
One race superior and another inferior
Is finally and permanently discredited
And abandoned
That until there are no longer
First class and second class citizens
Of any nation
Until the colour of a man's skin
Is of no more significance than
The colour of his eyes
That until the basic human rights
Are equally guaranteed to all
Without regard to race
That until that day
The dream of lasting peace, world citizenship
And the rule of international morality
Will remain in but a fleeting illusion
To be pursued, but never attained
And until the ignoble and unhappy
Regime that now hold our brothers
In Angola, in Mozambique, South Africa
In sub-human bondage, have been
Toppled and utterly destroyed
Until that day the African continent
Will not know peace
We Africans will fight, if necessary
And we know we shall win
As we are confident in the victory
Of good over evil, of good over evil."

("War"—based on speech by H.I.M. Haile Selassie I,
California, 28th February 1968)

*　　*　　*

In an interview with author Whitney, Mrs. Cedella Booker remembered early discussions with her son about Rastafari.

MLW: When Bob came to Delaware, was he showing signs of having sighted Rastafari?

CB: From him come there, that was when he was eighteen. He came there and he told me in the kitchen, he said momma, everything you cook is alright but me can't eat the pork. That time me used to cook bacon for me husband and meself, you understand, and him say me can't eat eggs either, him no like it and me say alright. But him used to tell me, you know, 'bout him no eat this and him no eat that and so I say what you eat and him say fish tea. And me say but fish tea alone can't keep you and him say yes and him say him make cornmeal porridge.

MLW: As a deeply rooted Christian woman, did you and Bob have discussions about Rastafari when it was something you weren't so conscious of?

CB: I used to pray and ask the Lord to change him because I said I am not a Rasta and I don't have anybody in the family who is a Rasta so why he come to be a Rasta. I always talk to God about it . . . but then at the time I was thinking God white [*laughter*]. So when he opened my eyes, then me realize and then me know, but Jah know me [was on the] right track, is only that I was of the wrong view and [Bob] was the one to open my eyes to reality. And he stay that night with me and he talk to me and he quote the scriptures and we were there reasoning from 9 o'clock the night after dinner until 3 o'clock the morning and he was telling me everything about His Majesty and him say you know why you [find it] hard to believe, is from you get up and you hear them talk about Jesus Christ and everything, it kinda hard for you to just come accept. But Jah say He is coming in a new name what sound so dreadful, which is Rastafari. [Bob] say you [are saying] to yourself, well you is a big woman and from you born come up you ask and you hear them talk 'bout Jesus Christ and to see your little son come tell you Jesus Christ is His Imperial Majesty, it sound a way to you, but then what is hidden from the wise and prudent is revealed to the babe and suckling still. You is a Rasta from a long time. From you born you is a Rasta, him used to tell me that for him want to see me really accept, and then I never oppose to nothing what he say.

MLW: I'm amazed to note how many people depend on you now for mothering. Where do you get so much strength?

CB: Jah, Jah give it to me. Bob give me a lot of strength, especially that morning him just give me everything. That morning when he blessed me before he departed. You know how some people feel holy, holy, holy. But I don't feel like that. I just feel like I was thirty-five, I mean I couldn't even tell you it now because maybe then I used to feel bad but now I'm feeling perfect.

"*I*s only one man me ask to make me be a servant unto HIM. Me no wan' do nothin' unless is HIM tell me to do it, you know. You hear what JAH say, 'until the philosophy which holds one race superior and another inferior . . .' No one else have nothin' more to write right now. Me no see nothin' great like that. People have to know that, and them have to know who say it. . . . You don't see that God Almighty say that? Watch where him come from—Africa . . . ."

(Marley, to Carl Gayle, *Black Music & Jazz Review*)

"Top Ranking, did you mean what you say now

CHAPTER 9

MUSICAL MESSAGE MASTER

*It's you, it's you, it's you I'm talking
to . . .
Why do you look so sad and
    forsaken
When one door is closed
Don't you know another is open*

("Coming In From The Cold")

F ANYONE had his doubts about the degree of Marley's commitment to his revolutionary message after hearing the unmilitant *Kaya* album in 1978, such doubts must surely have been dispelled when news of the One Love Peace Concert that same year rocked the world.

The concert was organized to celebrate a Peace Treaty which had been established by rival political gang leaders Claude Massop (of the Jamaica Labour Party) and Bucky Marshall (the People's National Party) to end the violent clashes which had turned Western Kingston into a terror-stricken war zone. Massop invited Marley to return home for the concert. Bob had not come back since the 1976 shooting incident.

It was an offer Bob would never have wanted to refuse. It was an indication that his brothers and sisters in the ghetto had finally realized what he had been trying to tell them all along: that they had a common enemy—the Babylon system of inequality and injustice. And that they could never overcome the system if they allowed those crazy baldheads who wielded power within it to manipulate them so that they consumed all their energy fighting each other instead of the true enemy.

Back them up, oh not the brothers,
But the ones who set them up . . .

("Time Will Tell")

The April 1978 One Love Peace Concert will be remembered as perhaps the best musicathon Jamaica has ever seen and will ever see. Among the performers who appeared were Oku Onuora, Culture, the Meditations, Dillinger, Leroy Smart, Althea and Donna, Dennis Brown, Lloyd Parks and We the People, Peter Tosh, Big Youth, and Ras Michael and Sons of Negus. It was a kind of homecoming for Marley.

Towards the end of the concert, Marley brought to centre stage, present Prime Minister Edward Seaga of the Jamaica Labour Party, then Leader of the Opposition, and the Prime Minister at the time, Michael Manley of the People's National Party; and these leaders of two opposing parties whose dislike of each other was extreme, shook hands that day in a promise for peace. It was an extraordinary moment. It became a hallmark reference to the stature of the man who had engineered it.

At the end of that year, Marley visited Africa for the first time. He went first to Kenya, then Ethiopia. Perhaps it was that visit which inspired him to

produce his most forceful album ever: *Survival*. Produced in 1979, *Survival* was the antithesis of *Kaya* in content. The theme was consistent, the tone stridently revolutionary. His message was a fusion and a culmination of all the components of the message which he had sung in the past. Rebellion, revolution, Rastafari righteousness prevailing; revelation, resolution, ultimate redemption.

Wake up and live now, he pleaded. Ignore the top ranking ones who were trying to keep the oppressed oppressed, "bribing with their guns, spare parts and money, trying to belittle our integrity" ("Ambush"). "Africa unite," he called, "it's later than you think" ("Africa Unite"). To the liberation forces of Zimbabwe he again pleaded for unity—"no more internal power struggle"—and chanted his support: "Mash it up in a Zimbabwe" ("Zimbabwe").

A Grand Array of Reggae Stars—who along with Bob Marley & The Wailers turned the 1978 Peace Concert at Jamaica's National Stadium into one of the greatest musical feasts of local history. Among them (opp. page from top): Dennis Brown, Jacob Miller, Big Youth; (this page from top) Leroy Sibbles, Althea & Donna and Culture. Jacob "Killer" Miller brought a real jovial mood to the occasion by cavorting his tons of fun and making his peace spliff offering. Miller was killed in a car accident in March 1980 on Hope Road in Kingston.

Bob in action at the One Love Peace Concert (above) and holding aloft the hands of the then Prime Minister, Michael Manley and Opposition Leader, Edward Seaga in a gesture of peace and unity. Below, newspaper front page tells its own story of the shooting incident two years earlier.

Rise ye mighty people
There is work to be done
So let's do it little by little
Rise from your sleepless slumber
We're more than the sand on the seashore
We're more than numbers

("Wake Up And Live")

To the Babylon oppressors he spewed forth cries of rage, songs of doom.

How can you be sitting there
Telling me that you care . . .
When everytime I look around
The people in suffering
In everywhere

("Survival")

Now the fire is burning
Out of control, panic in the city . . .
Destroying and melting their gold
Destroying and wasting their souls . . .
Now the people gather on the beach
And the leader try to make a speech
But dread again tell them it's too late

("Ride Natty Ride")

124

And for the oppressed peoples of the world, the lingering message was one of certain retribution, a redressing of wrongs.

> **I know Jah would never let us down**
> **Pull your rights from wrong . . .**
> **Starvation dread dread . . .**
> **Lamentation dread dread**
> **But read it in revelation . . .**
> **You'll find your redemption**
>
> ("One Drop")

> **In this age of technological inhumanity**
> **We're the survivors, black survival**
> **Scientific atrocity, we're the survivors**
> **Atomic mis-philosophy, we're the survivors**
>
> ("Survival")

The songs of Robert Nesta Marley were recorded chapters of his biography; they were like lessons from the trials and tribulations he had experienced and witnessed over the years. Once spoken in song the option of being able to hear them again and again probably reinforced his determination to help his brothers and sisters to travel on a straight path of righteousness, avoiding pitfalls and unnecessary detours.

Like David with his slingshot, and Samson with the jawbone of an ass, Marley used his musical instrument—the voice—as a tool to conquer the odds. "Greetings in the name of His Imperial Majesty Haile I Selassie, Jah Rastafari, Ever Living, Ever Faithful, Ever Sure," was the live and continuously living testimonial that was so deeply embedded it could no longer be contained—it was shouted out at the start of all Marley performances. It always brought a reaction that was so enthusiastic and sincere that one could hardly doubt that the King of Reggae had arrived.

Marley's music, live or recorded, arrested the listener, and helped him to question his traditional values and replace them with the realities of Marley's songs. The effect was mesmerizing. Many hung on to his every word as the instruction for the liberation of their souls. His songs were solace and comfort to the wounded, the sick, the infirm of heart; those disillusioned with things as they are and trying to cling or to hold on to the promise of a new day.

Reggae has been described many times as heartbeat music. It has a definite pulse of its own. When the heart is attacked rhythmically the way it always is by the music of Bob Marley and the Wailers, the listener just gets carried away.

> *"Through political strategy*
> *They keep us hungry*
> *And when you gonna get some food*
> *Your brother got to be your enemy."*
> **(Ambush)**

125

There was life support in all of Marley's songs; they served as a righteous respirator for anyone in doubt. Bob Marley transmitted a kind of kinetic energy to which thousands and thousands, hundreds of thousands lined up to be connected. The force was truly with him. And he put it all out there. To really appreciate Bob Marley and the Wailers full employment of all the senses was required and they had to work overtime.

**We refuse to be
What you wanted us to be
We are what we are
That's the way it's going to be
You can't educate I
For no equal opportunity
Talkin' 'bout my freedom
People freedom and liberty
We've been trodding on
The winepress much too long
Rebel, rebel**

("Babylon System")

PRESENTED BY
THE GOVERNMENT
AND PEOPLE
OF THE REPUBLIC
OF NIGERIA

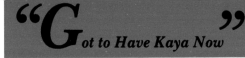

Actual figures for Bob Marley albums sales could never be fully assessed for reasons most reggae artistes are all too familiar with. The calculations are done by a unique set of rules that somehow always seem to balance the books to the benefit of the producer.

Estimates at the time of his passing would say that earnings from Bob Marley's record sales ran in excess of 200 million dollars. The general opinion is that if that is the figure that was volunteered, then you can add considerably to it for a picture of what a valuable commodity the music messenger was. And by now the figures must have quadrupled.

From America to Zimbabwe in that special record rack marked "Roots, Rock, Reggae", its leading exponent was always out front. And there was no language barrier, for Bob Marley spoke in a universal tongue.

Ever on the peace path, Marley's music sent smoke signals that were picked up by his brown brothers, the Hava Supai, a tribe of Indians who reside in North America. Film director Jo Menell, while researching footage for a documentary film on Marley produced by Chris Blackwell, met with these Indians and shares his encounter:

JM: At the bottom of the Grand Canyon in the United States of America, there is a tribe, a nation of American Indians called the Hava Supai [People of the Blue Water] and these people from the early 70s onward [have been listening to] the music of Bob Marley. They have listened to everything that Bob ever sang and everybody down there has a small tape recorder and there is always a Bob Marley tape in that. They actually believe that Bob is a prophet and that he is alive and that he is talking to them. And when I heard that, I figured that was something to check out, so I went there alone and met with the Indians and I hadn't been down there but a few hours before I realized that this was much bigger than I had imagined.

Now the Indians allowed nobody to film them, they're against filming and turned down every possible offer. Over a month before, Henry Fonda wanted to make a film down there because the location is stunning. You're at the bottom of the Grand Canyon with mile-high cliffs, you've got three of the most beautiful waterfalls you have ever seen and an Indian tribe. Fonda wrote them a blank check and said fill it in and then we're in business and they said no. I went down there and talked to them about this film and they said well it's

Left: A tall measure of appreciation was presented to Bob by the Nigerian government. Mamadou Johnny Sekka from Senegal looks on.

a wonderful idea, but we don't allow filming. Maybe if we put it to the full tribal counsel we'll see. So I had to appear in front of the full tribal counsel of seven very elderly *dreads* (which is the only way I could describe them because they were definitely dreads with their hair down to the ground) and I simply said that the film I wanted to make was a film about Bob Marley and the Indians' identification with him and why they identified with him, I would like to get their views on that. They then debated in front of me for about an hour in the Supai language which I understood nothing of and in the end the unanimous answer was yes, which says something for Bob. I was just the messenger on this. Then, having decided that, they laid down several conditions, the first of which was that they see the final film when it was made because they would love to see a film on Bob Marley, and I gave them a written guarantee that I would be back with the final film and show it and take a projector down.

The second one was, if I came to film they would like to meet some Rastafarians . . . I said yes to that not knowing quite how I would organize that but I felt somewhere I could find some good Rastas who would see the point of going there. And those were the basic conditions. Well, when I discussed this with Chris Blackwell and Rita Marley, in the end it was decided I'd go back down there, and Mrs. Booker [Bob's mother] came with me, and Tyrone Downie [Wailers keyboardist] and the effect of their arrival was just something you would have to see to believe. I mean they were welcomed as messengers from Bob and the Indians responded to them in an extraordinary way. We spent three days down there filming.

MLW: How were they reflecting on the effect Bob's music had on them? Did they speak with Mrs. Booker?

JM: Oh, absolutely, they wanted to know about Rasta, they wanted to know about Jamaica. And on the film you will see the actual Indians saying remarkable things like Jah and Barkiova. Barkiova is the name they have which means the great spirit and they say Jah and Barkiova is one and the same God. They believe in Jah because they know that he must be the same as theirs. So there's this identification not just on the human rights level. I mean, their favourite songs are "Chase Those Crazy Baldheads", "Get Up Stand Up", "400 Years", not just that but it was on a spiritual level too, which was a really remarkable thing.

In 1979 Bob Marley and the Wailers embarked on the most extensive tour of their history, taking Bob's message beyond North America and Europe to such distant countries as Japan, Australia and Hawaii. And the following year there was another world tour. But this one was probably the most significant of all for Bob—not only because it would prove to be his last, but because it started in Africa. Gabon first, then Zimbabwe, where blood brother Bob Marley had been invited to sing songs of freedom at the country's official independence ceremony.

Zimbabwe, formerly known as Southern Rhodesia, had been under minority British colonial rule for nearly a century. If polled, Marley's musical followers would surely vote unanimously that his contribution to the celebrations surrounding the ascent of the freedom flag of Zimbabwe under the new leadership of Prime Minister.

Robert Mugabe was one of his biggest triumphs. It was a great honour, and it demonstrated his importance to the Third World.

April 17, 1980 will leave an indelible mark in the history of the independence struggles of all African nations.

> So arm in arms, with arms
> We will fight this little struggle
> 'Cos that's the only way
> We can overcome our little trouble
> Brother you're right, you're right . . .
> We gonna fight
> We'll have to fight . . .
> Fight for our rights . . .
> Divide and rule
> Could only tear us apart
> In every man's chest
> There beats a heart
> So soon we'll find out
> Who is the real revolutionary
> And I don't want my people
> To be tricked by mercenaries

("Zimbabwe")

Dera Tompkins, an African American radio personality, was in Zimbabwe when Bob Marley and the Wailers arrived. She described it as "a definite act of Jah . . ."

"I think being in Zimbabwe at that time was personally for Bob, the highest point. I mean no honourable mention or order of merit, no other moment could have been as significant. The *Survival* album with the song "Zimbabwe" had nearly become an anthem. No other entertainer outside of Zimbabwe was invited to perform, not even from the continent of Africa. All of the performances during the celebrations were by Zimbabweans. It had been more than twenty years since any entertainer had come. The airport was the site of a beautiful reunion. If I had to title it I would call it "Zion By Bus," because a bus picked up the Wailers at the airport.

"In town there were banners saying 'Welcome to Zimbabwe' and announcing the independence celebrations and it was 'Viva Zimbabwe' and everyone's spirit and heart was into it. And from that moment the excitement continued to heighten and truly manifest."

Judy Mowatt of the I Threes related the experience in an interview with author Whitney.

JM: We were told that these people were in the hills, in the bush for years because of fighting. Now because of the Independence everyone had gotten the liberty of coming to the streets and coming to the forefront. So they were like fowls who were locked up in a coop for a long time and you let them out. Everybody was just walking, walking, I don't even think they even knew where they were going but just the freedom of walking on the street. When we got to where we were staying, the soil I tell you, the soil look so different. Rich. The place is similar to Jamaica. I must tell you this, every fruit tree that we have in Jamaica, the beaches and everything same, so you know Jamaica is really a part of Africa. So when we go there it wasn't anything too surprising. The

SALISBURY CELEBRATES

INDEPENDENT ZIMBABWE 18th APRIL, 1980

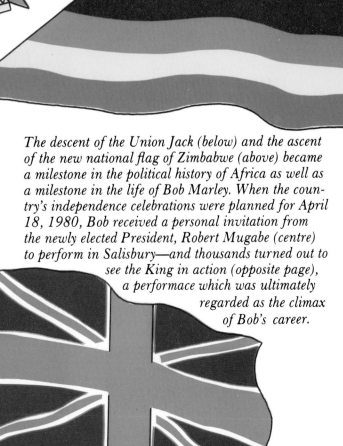

> "The hotter the battle
> The sweeter Jah victory."
> (Heathen)

The descent of the Union Jack (below) and the ascent of the new national flag of Zimbabwe (above) became a milestone in the political history of Africa as well as a milestone in the life of Bob Marley. When the country's independence celebrations were planned for April 18, 1980, Bob received a personal invitation from the newly elected President, Robert Mugabe (centre) to perform in Salisbury—and thousands turned out to see the King in action (opposite page), a performace which was ultimately regarded as the climax of Bob's career.

discrimination that the people face with the white people was different. We met some people and they were telling us how they suffered in the bush. A little girl, she couldn't be more than ten, she was telling us how while in the bush she had to manoeuvre herself, she had to carry a gun, because her hair is cut down like a boy and she had to watch her little sisters and brothers die and they have to quickly find a hole for them, to bury them before the enemies come and find that there is a trail of people. So she had to make haste and draw them and bury them and run again. This little girl, her ears were like a dog because she's so sensitive that when she talk to you you see her ears kept going up like a puppy's when she hears a sound, and she's looking both sides like she don't trust no one, and anybody that come on, she scrutinize them from head to foot. This was really a different sort of life because in Jamaica when you check it, you really have freedom compared to what these people have gone through, and their way of life is just brutal.

Bob stayed [in Zimbabwe] and he got a feel of the place, to reason with the people, to know how them feel, and even with his song the people said that while they were going through the struggle and the war, the fighting and the killing, for the women it was the song "No

"Sons and daughters will rise again to fulfill the goals of the revolution . . ."
(**Essence**, July 1981)

Woman, No Cry" that gave them consolation and strength to go through, and generally the song "Zimbabwe" was what really motivated the soldiers to know that we'll have to fight, fight, fight for our rights and even if one die we never really give up because this is something we have to do to overcome the trouble that we're going through.

MLW: Did that stage feel different, looking out at Rufaro Stadium? How would you describe that feeling?

JM: Well, the feeling that I got, the vibration was more intense; is black people, not much white people and not that I'm discriminating against white people. . . . I was taught and for myself I believe in three races, the white man, the brown man and the black man. 'Cos if you check the white in your eyes, it has brown, it has black and it has white and His Majesty say not until the colour of man's skin is of no more significance than the colour of his eyes. If you look in our eyes, the three of them is there together and if you should separate one then you would spoil the whole eye. But as black woman now, I am saying that it was really good for me to experience this, to be in a stadium with all black people and not all of us speaking the same language but all of us sharing the same struggles, and they can identify, even if they don't understand the words of what we are singing, the intensity of the message, they can see the determination in what we are saying and that's the same thing we are sharing, the determination in overcoming. The real objective or what we are aspiring for, is to overcome; so when they saw us, they really saw that this is another part of us come together. One half was in the west and this part here, we came together. So really it was a reunion.

MLW: There was a report of some disturbance which involved teargassing?

JM: What had happened is that the soldiers who were responsible for the liberation and independence of Zimbabwe were not invited to that ceremony, the ceremonial dance and everything. They were not invited and Bob Marley is a lover of everyone there. So they heard that Bob Marley was there and everyone wanted to come. Well, while we were on stage they were about 250 kilometers away from the stage and they heard the music. The airwaves took it over to them and it was like they were in a trance and they were just following the sound and it led them right to the stadium.

MLW: An ital piper.

JM: And they came barging in and a lot of soldiers [of the former Rhodesian government] were there, [and] if you saw that place you would think this is a war zone, you know it's a war zone but you think that war would break out any time and you say Lord, My God, what we come down here for, I wonder if we come down here to kill off we self. You see the tankers and the white soldiers, but most of them came to protect Prince Charles and people were coming, coming . . . .

MLW: I didn't know that the Prince was there?

JM: Well yes, he came to represent his mother, the Queen, because she didn't make it. Anyway, they kept coming, coming . . . . When the people barge in the soldiers tell them you are not invited, you are uninvited guests, you have to get back. So they started to fight their way in because if them could fight their way to make that independence possible them have to fight them way to come in to hear the one who give the strength and consolation to go through, to overcome. The soldiers began now to teargas the place. I started smelling a strange sensation and it was burning and your eyes was burning and you start coughing and you can't sing but you find that you suffocated. Now when I look 'round I wonder if is me one feeling this, when I look I see Rita and I see Marcia and they looking like them have the same feeling so we step back from the mike and begin to cough. And then we look [and] we see poor Bob, 'cause when him sing him is always in a trance and he's millions, millions of miles away from where we are, because we are there watching physically and him was way, way up, but you can see that him had come down and him wondering what is happening and him want to sing but he was unable to sing, him just step back and people come to lead Ziggy and Stephen [Bob's children] off stage and the musicians was coughing and everybody moving. And I say, I wonder if is really the war starting now. I wonder if is die we going to die down here in Zimbabwe now, because a whole lot of things hit you now because you are miles and miles from your children.

And we still didn't know what had happened so we went into a trailer, but even the trailer couldn't keep out the intoxication of the teargas that was seeping in through the crevices. We pass little children fainting and you couldn't help them. You saw children knocked out on the ground and you wonder if is dead them dead but you don't know what is happening and you want to try to save yourself. 'Cos when trouble like those surround you, you just think to save yourself and everybody is saying, where Bob, but you still trying to protect yourself. And we saw this brother Joe Stebleski who was here in Jamaica and we ask him to drive us to the place where we were staying and when we got there, we were in our costumes and watching the whole thing on the TV and we saw when the Union Jack came down and they were putting up the new flag. We wanted to be there 'cos the musicians were there and Bob was still there, and Rita said to Joe Stebleski that she want to go back to see what is happening to Bob and she is not leaving until she know what is taking place with Bob. I mean she have to leave the place where she's at to go where he is.

When she go she say she see them just come off and Bob look at her and say, "Now I know who are the true revolutionaries."

MLW: Serious?

JM: Wha' you mean? When you talk about determination, will and faith to do whatever he is sent to do, it is that man. I think that if I have learned anything, I have learned the sense of trying to perfect things to its greatest heights, I've learned to be patient and I have learned to be determined to fight for whatever is right, and whatever you are doing that is right, if is even crocheting, you know that it is something that is worthwhile seeing, it is going to give you self-satisfaction. Sometimes you can't get no right stitches, you get it and it don't fit in and something wrong with it; crocheting is like people, if it's not formulated in that right and proper pattern then it can't look as how it's supposed to look. And then you have to pull the threads if is even to start it all over again, it has to be uniform, so that is what I have learned from [Bob]. Whatever you are doing there must be a vast amount of determination to fulfill.

"Death can always take life from you but never will it take away what you've created in your life."

Wise men in the village used to say that in Africa. Once again they are right, for the news spread by Bob Marley has fallen over the continent. Yes, they are right, because Bob may not be still on earth but his messages still remain. Thus he achieved his aim which was to spread the Rasta message all over the world. Why should we cry for him? With all that we received from the message. We should have to weep, cry, if the message was lost, but it isn't, so we just have to rejoice, to give some praise to the most high, and dance to Jah music in Zion. That's the way the Africans paid tribute to one of the Rasta messengers: BOB MARLEY.

In Ivory Coast, West Africa, all the ghetto of Abidjan [Capital of Ivory Coast] was in a kind of meditation, a kind of Nyabinghi [Rasta Bredren Reunion]. People were awake in the streets, day and night, forgetting for about two weeks the existence of the sun and the moon. In Williams Ville, North Abidjan, a young Rasta association organized a special Bob Marley night during which they listened to all the records of the Wailers, by candlelight. Meanwhile, in the streets of the town, some local musicians holding torches were moving from one section to another, creating a massive human energy flow simply by means of unity. Unity that all the black people need, to fight together, to live in peace, love and harmony. "When one builds a hospital to avoid death, one always foresees a mortuary, we know that very well, that means there is a necessary sacrifice to have access to victory," said Tiama, a 16-year-old boy, as he danced his way towards the torch-lit crowd.

In the air, Bob's voice coming from either radio sets or record players, vibrated the cars. "Zion train is coming our way" was the favourite sentence that people repeated strongly with hands up, like a magical recital. So was the atmosphere till the daylight came, and Abidjan was sparkling with the "uprising sun" now like it had never been before. Spreading over the town was a kind of "natural mystic" in the air that brings people to accept the reality of nature.

A short TV programme started in the afternoon retracing the life of the singer, and catching all the attention of spectators, as much for the dreadlock hair style as Bob's speech. For a few days after, several Rasta shows went on, giving the opportunity to different singers to pay tribute to Bob in their own way, dressing in Bob effigy T-shirts, elevating the faithful from the homage shown to their brother. The ambiance was so alive that it seemed to me that I was once more experiencing the "International Year of the Rasta Child" show that I attended in August 1979 at the National Arena in Kingston (Jamaica). The walls of many inhabitants had been scratched with drawings and scripts about Bob and the Rasta philosophy: "Bob is not Jamaican, he is African," "the Rasta will win", "tribute to his Imperial Majesty Haile Selassie", "this district quarter is named Zion City", "Here is Jah people city", "Jah no dead", "Rastafari".

How could I say it was a funeral, because funerals reflect death, but in this case it was like a feast. When reflecting on the reaction of the Ivorians about Bob Marley, I just say that they have understood the Rasta message, all of it. As the young Abdoul (12 years old) of the ghetto of Adjame [center of Abidjan] told me, "They used our physical energy, they sold many parts of our culture, they left us in poverty, but never will they take from us the reason of our existence: the promised land, Zion." Rest in peace, Bob, we understood the message.

KONE BARU OMAR
Ivory Coast
September 1981 (Translated)

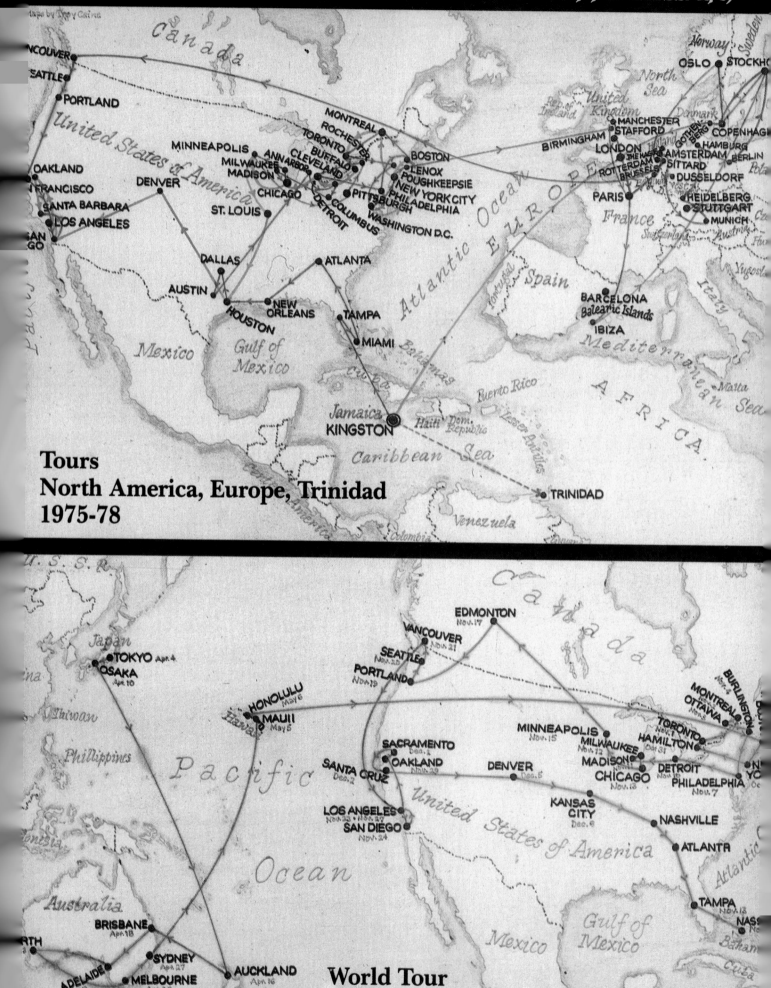

**Tours
North America, Europe, Trinidad
1975-78**

**World Tour
1979**

PROVIDENCE R.I. Sept. 17 · Sept. 16

NEW YORK Sept. 19

PITTSBURGH Sept. 22

United States of America

North Atlantic Ocean

Caribbean Sea · JAMAICA

Portugal · *Spain*

BARCELONA June 30

GLASGOW July 10 · *North Sea*

Norway June 16 · STOCKHOLM

Sweden

Repub. of Ireland · *United Kingdom*

DUBLIN July 6 · DEESIDE July 12

STAFFORD July 13

COPENHAGEN June 18

Denmark

HAMBURG June 14

East Germany

LONDON June 7 · ROTTERDAM June 23

BRIGHTON July 8 · DORTMUND June 15

WEST BERLIN June 19

LILLE June 24 · KASSEL June 20 · *Poland*

PARIS July 3 · BRUSSELS June 22 · COLOGNE June 15

NANTES July 2 · KAISERSLAUTERN June 8

ORLEANS June 10 · STRASBOURG June 9 · *Czechoslovakia*

DIJON · MUNICH June 1 · *Austria*

BORDEAUX June 11 · ZURICH May 30 · *Hungary*

GRENOBLE June 3 · MILAN June 27 · *Italy*

TURIN June 26 · *Yugoslavia*

TOULON June 26

World Tour 1980

Below: Bob with manager Don Taylor and friends, showing off two of his many gold albums.

Africa

LIBREVILLE Jan. 5 · *Gabon*

South Atlantic Ocean

SALISBURY Apr. 18 · *Zimbabwe*

DISCOGRAPHY

SINGLES

BLUE MOUNTAIN:
Baby We've Got A Date / Stop That Train
BULLET:
Soultown / Let The Sun Shine On Me
Lick Samba / Samba *(Beverley's)*
CBS:
Reggae on Broadway / Oh Lord I Got To Get There
CLOCKTOWER:
Duppy Conqueror / Duppy Version
COXSONE:
Dancing Time / Treat Me Good *(Peter Tosh & The Wailers)*
Rudie / Rudie Part Two *(Bob Marley and a Studio One band)*
I'm Still Waiting / Ska Jerk
DOCTOR BIRD:
Rude Boy / Ringo's Theme (This Boy) *(B-side: Roland Alphonso and The Soul Brothers)*
Nice Time / Hypocrite
Good Good Rudie / Oceans 11 *(B-side: The City Slickers)*
Rasta Put It On / Ska With Ringo *(A-side: Peter Tosh & The Wailers; B-side: Roland Alphonso)*
ESCORT:
To The Rescue / Run For Cover
GREEN DOOR:
Trench Town Rock / Grooving Kingdom
Lively Up Yourself / Live: Tommy McCook *(produced by Marley)*
Guava Jelly / Redder Than Red *(produced by Marley)*
ISLAND:
Judge Not / Do You Still Love Me
One Cup of Coffee / Judge Not *(B-side: The Skatalites)*
One Cup of Coffee / Exodus *(B-side: Ernest Ranglin)*
It Hurts To Be Alone / Mr. Talkative
Playboy / Your Love
Hoot Nanny Hoot / Do You Remember *(Peter Tosh & The Wailers)*
Hooligan / Maga Dog
Shame And Scandal / The Jerk *(Peter Tosh & The Wailers)*
Don't Ever Leave Me / Donna
What's New Pussycat / What Will I Find
Independent Anniversary Ska (I Should Have Known Better) / Jumble Jamboree *(A-side: The Skatalites)*
Put It On / Love Won't Be Mine
He Who Feels It Knows It / Sunday Morning
Rude Boy Get Bail (Let Him Go) / Sinner Man
Bend Down Low / Freedom Time
I Am The Toughest / No Faith *(A-side: Peter Tosh; B-side: Marcia Griffiths)*
Concrete Jungle / Reincarnated Souls
Get Up Stand Up / Slave Driver
So Jah Seh / Natty Dread
No Woman No Cry / Kinky Reggae *(Live at The Lyceum)*
Jah Lives / Concrete
Johnny Was (Woman Hang Your Head Down Low) / Cry To Me
Roots Rock Reggae / Stir It Up
Follow Fashion Monkey / Instr. *(U.S. release only)*
I Shot The Sheriff / Pass It On / Duppy Conqueror *(D.J. only)*
Exodus / Wait In Vain *(D.J. only—with Marley talking)*
Exodus / Instr. • Waiting In Vain / Roots
Jamming / Punky Reggae Party • Is This Love / Crisis Version
Satisfy My Soul / Smile Jamaica
War / No More Trouble / Exodus *(Limited edition: taken from 'Babylon By Bus')*
So Much Trouble / Instr. • Zimbabwe / Survival
Africa Unite / Wake Up And Live
Could You Be Loved / One Drop / Ride Natty Ride
Three Little Birds / Every Need Got An Ego To Feed
Redemption Song / Band Version • I Shot The Sheriff *(Live 12")*
Stir It Up / Rat Race *(Live)*
Survival / Wake Up And Live
JACKPOT:
Mr. Chatterbox / Walk Through The World
PUNCH:
Small Axe / What A Confusion *(B-side: Dave Barker)*
Downpresser / Got The Tip *(B-side: Junior Bytes)*
You Should Have Known Better • Screwface / Faceman

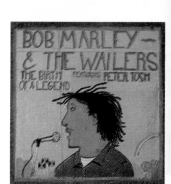

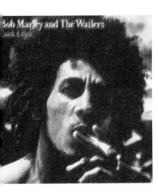

RIO:
Dancing Shoes / Don't Look Back
Pied Piper / It's Alright (B-side: Rita Marley)
You Lied / Crawfish (A-side: Rita Marley; B-side: Soul Brothers)

SKABEAT:
Simmer Down / I Don't Need Your Love
Train To Skaville / I Made A Mistake (A side: Soul Brothers)
Love And Affection / Teenager In Love
And I Love Her / Do It Right • Lonesome Track / Zimmerman
Lonesome Feelings / There She Goes

SMASH:
Stop The Train / Caution • Freedom Train

SUMMIT:
Stop The Train / Caution (Beverley's)

TROJAN:
Stir It Up / This Train • Soul Shakedown Party / Shakedown Version
But I Do / Your Love • Soul Shakedown Party / Caution
Mr. Brown / Trenchtown Rock

TUFF GONG:
Lick Samba / Samba • Rat Race / Part Two
Smile Jamaica Parts One And Two
Work / Guided Missile (Produced by A. Barrett)
Roots Rock Reggae / War • Exodus / Instr.
A Jah Jah / Jah Version (Bob & Rita Marley)
Rastaman Live Up / Don't Give Up • Blackman Redemption / Version
Hypocrite / Nice Time • Ambush / Ambush In Dub
One Drop / One Dub • Comin' In From The Cold / Dubbin' In
Punky Reggae Party • Knotty Dread / Version
Craven Choke Puppy / Choke (Wailers All Stars)
Satisfy My Soul Jah Jah / Version (The Wailers Group)
Many Are Called (The I-Threes) • Put It On (Judy Mowatt)
Nice Time • Man To Man (Rita Marley) • Talking Blues • Road Block
Belly Full • What An Experience (Judy Mowatt) • Thank You Lord (Rita Morley)
You Pour Sugar On Me (Judy Mowatt)
Eastern Memphis (Family Man & The Rebel Arms) • Mr. Big Man (J. Mowatt)
Medley (The I-Threes) • Black Woman (Judy Mowatt)
The Beauty of God's Plan (Rita Marley) • Bad Card • I Know (45 Disco)
Trodding (Melody Makers) • Children Playing (Melody Makers)

UPSETTER:
My Cup / Son Of Thunder (B-side: Lee Perry & The Upsetters)
Duppy Conqueror / Justice • Mr. Brown / Dracula (B-side: The Upsetters)
Kaya / Version (B-side: The Upsetters) • Small Axe / All In One
Picture On The Wall / Picture Version (A-side: Rass Dawkins & The Wailers; B-side: The Upsetters)
More Axe / Axe Man • Dream Land / Version (B-side: The Upsetters)
More Axe / The Axe Man (B-side: The Upsetters)
Keep On Moving / African Herbsman

LABEL UNKNOWN:
Second Hand • Jah Is Might

ALBUMS

JAMAICAN ALBUMS:
The Wailing Wailers (Studio One/Coxsone)
The Best Of Bob Marley & The Wailers (Studio One/Coxsone)
Present Soul Revolution Part Two (Maroon/Upsetters)
Present Soul Revolution Part Three Maroon/Upsetters)
The Best Of The Wailers (Beverley's)

TROJAN:
Soul Rebels • African Herbsman • Rasta Revolution

ISLAND/TUFFGONG:
Catch A Fire • Burnin' • Natty Dread • Rastaman Vibration
Live! (British release Only) • A Taste Of The Wailers (Limited edition d.j. Br. release only)
Exodus • Kaya • Babylon By Bus • Survival • Uprising

CBS:
Birth Of A Legend Parts 1 & 2 (Studio One songs)

ALBUM CAPSULE REVIEWS

by DERMOTT HUSSEY

CHANCES ARE is a welcome collector's item, revealing much that hitherto had been unreleased, or if not, out of print. The songs were recorded from 1968 through 1972 and come from a period of association between the Wailers, Danny Simms and Johnny Nash. Some of the remixing is muddy with a "new" musical overlay that does not always succeed, but of the times that it does, of which there are many, the title track stands out as the gem of the collection. A plaintive song in a R&B style or what Jamaicans call a "soft tune", "Chances are some might not hold out" gives the lyrics an autobiographical ring.

Catch A Fire's release in 1973 was the launching of international reggae. It struck responsive chords among oppressed peoples, with such classics as "Concrete Jungle", "Slave Driver" and "400 Years". The music shows a strong foreign influence in musicianship and instrumentation.

BURNIN' is significant; though this album was recorded at the same time as *Catch a Fire*, it contributed in more roots terms towards a message that had begun years before. It shows revolutionary fervour fused with Rastafarian spiritualism, which had been embraced by the Wailers at that time. It has two sermons by Bunny Wailer, "Pass It On" and "Hallelujah Time", as well as new arrangements of older hits, "Put it On", "Small Axe" and "Duppy Conqueror". It was also the last album done by the original Wailers.

NATTY DREAD is Marley's debut album as a solo artiste, and a work of classical proportions. It has incredible lyrical strength and beauty, supported by unforgettable musicianship, and became a definitive work with regard to what was described as the sound of reggae. "No Woman No Cry" is a one-of-a-kind reggae song, and every other track except "Bend Down Low" is steaming with Marley's steely defiance. The introduction of the I Threes was a brilliant stroke, and their expert harmonies gave the music a fullness that soon became characteristic.

RASTAMAN VIBRATION is a departure from the form of "Natty Dread", and finds Bob reaching for wider audiences and fields of appreciation. The previous position of uncompromising Rastafari belief is widened to include more varied material, some original, some re-recorded. As a singer, Marley's style began to assimilate subtle stylistic effects of jazz and pop phrasing. The critics, being often no more than barometers of their own bias rather than any representation of the people's taste, began criticizing Marley's attempts to gain wider popularity, and concomitantly the similar attempts of reggae itself, which were, they deemed, at the expense of the music remaining pure.

EXODUS, Marley's bestseller, is an emotional album, and with good reason. An attempt was made on Marley's life and the singer went into exile for over a year, his ego wounded. The first side of the album is a complete statement in response to that event. He interprets much of that experience through the wisdom and teachings of the Bible, but at the same time his criticisms are trenchant. The five-part chapter concludes with a triumphant soul-stirring "Exodus". The second side is celebratory, delving into love songs, a previously unheard of preoccupation, at least on a sustained basis in militant reggae, but an important side of Marley's writing. Some of the sentiments are predictably familiar, but Marley does bring more than accustomed clichés to most of the love songs, as say in "Turn Your Lights Down Low" and in the kind of love he is dealing with in "One Love".

Kaya Every album released by Bob Marley was developmental, and it is possible to trace a very clear path of development from *Natty Dread*, his first as a solo artist. *Kaya* is no less in this regard. It follows *Exodus* which began to bring Marley to a wider audience in his singular attempt to extend the boundaries of the music he had come to symbolize. *Kaya* is a departure from the militant fervour.

In his search for a wider audience, and in creating a more accessible music, Bob is more carefree. The songs probe runnings that are more diverse. Lyrically they run between observations about easy skanking, ganja, love, and some of the natural elements that are always present in his writing: the rising and the shining sun, for example, suggesting the days he spent at Nine Miles, which is the mood of "Sun Is Shining." "Running Away" questions his reasons for going into exile after the attempt on his life in 1976. He asks himself whether by running away he really ran away from himself.

Musically, Marley is adventurous. His singing is more relaxed, employs jazz phrasing and is a conscious attempt to broaden his range. The Wailers bubble in a tight groove under the musical orders of Aston Barrett's one drop bass, and his brother Carly's cantering sock cymbal accents. Junior Marvin, the guitarist, adds some nice touches throughout, particularly his twelve-string in "Time Will Tell".

SURVIVAL

While *Kaya* was in some ways an extension of the B side of *Exodus,* and a bestseller, *Survival* was a sharp reminder for the critics and those who take them seriously, that in no way had Marley's revolutionary fervour waned, nor had he gone soft. It was an instant classic replete with some of his best writing. "Babylon System" is a brilliant and moving work whose telling lyrics are passionately related over a 'burru' beat. "Zimbabwe" is relentless and driving with Marley answering an implied conversation, "Brother you're so right, we'll have to fight," committing Natty irrevocably to the struggle. In comparison, "Africa Unite" is an urgent plea, for "as it has been said, let it be done." Closer to home in "Top Ranking" he confronts the powers that continually pit the people against themselves.

In *Survival* he pays tribute to the black race that suffers still but survives in spite of it all, and he cautions us to "Wake Up And Live" nevertheless. In "One Drop", he eschews the tendency of the people of Africa to be controlled by either of the political "isms", which despite their individual virtues have been unable to stop the people from fighting or dying from hunger and starvation. Instead he wants the teachings of Africa to prevail: "Give us the teachings of His Majesty, we don't want no devil philosophy." He stings with "Ambush In The Night", referring to Jamaica's political rivalry and the attendant bribery of "guns, spare parts and money."

UPRISING

is the summation of an era which began with Marley's rise in 1975. It achieves a perfect balance between serious lyrics and an assured music that does its job so well. It was as if Marley had perfected the technique of giving serious music commercial clout without sacrificing its inherent qualities. For example, "Real Situation" and "We And Them" are serious comments but their respective musical accompaniment is so deft that the songs take on a different character to that originally suggested, as is the case in "Could You Be Loved", whose very title is deceptive by virtue of its musical context. "Redemption Song" is possibly the best song Marley wrote and ironically one of his last. It is cast in a familiar mould, the apocalyptic vision, at which Marley had already excelled. From its first chord of guitar accompaniment, Marley sings for all those who had "taken up the mantle and gone before," singing a song of freedom; sings the same song for us now in this generation; and sings for those to follow:

> Emancipate yourselves from mental slavery
> None but ourselves can free our minds
> Have no fear of atomic energy
> 'Cause none of them can stop the time

CONFRONTATION

is the new album released in 1983, two years after Bob's death. It contains five tracks never before released in any form, four previously released only in Jamaica. In this album the message is divided between exhorting the good to overcome the forces of evil (Babylon) with haunting supplications to JAH. From the beautiful "Give Thanks and Praises" and the passionate "I Know" to the catchy "Buffalo Soldier", this is Marley at his best, and through it all his deepest convictions shine through strongly.

> Many a time I sit and wonder
> why the race so, so very hard to run
> Then I say to my soul
> Take courage
> Battle to be won . . . .
> ("I Know")

CHAPTER 10

A RASTAMAN'S VIBRATIONS

One love, one heart
Let's get together and feel alright

("One Love")

UPON leaving Zimbabwe, Bob Marley and the Wailers set out on an extended European tour, covering some thirty European cities from Barcelona to Oslo, from West Berlin to Dublin. In Milan the show was a sellout, with over 100,000 fans attending. From city to city the band moved like a raging fire, breaking show attendance records made by major rock groups, including the Beatles and the Rolling Stones.

Bob Marley as a live performer was an event. His inspiration and power, his dynamism and charisma, made his presence on stage much larger than the physical dimensions.

At the best of those performances, the audience, a willing partner in such moments, seemed aware that something unusual was taking place. Many reports speak of Bob becoming entranced while the music lifted him away from the immediate surroundings to wherever such fortunate souls are privileged to go. He fell often and hurt himself, not because he was high, though indeed he often was, but because he had so completely surrendered to the music. His boundless energy was apparent from when he was a young performer. Then, it is said, he got so carried away that he regularly fell right off the stage. For instance there is an early photograph of Bob's head bandaged on just such an occasion. He once said, resting after a long tour, "I work so hard till I sweat inna me shoes."

He was a natural for the world of pop that is built on a pre-planned promotional slick for emotion and a formula for live presentation. Marley had intensity and urgency which came bubbling over a rhythm of such locomotive power that it spoke to the feet. He brought a new vocabulary to the language of live performance: flashing locks, Nyabinghi shuffles, and other moves spontaneously created, such as the apocalyptic pointing finger that inspired British critic Karl Dallas to liken him to Bob Dylan.

Someone who has seen Marley's live performance more than most is Neville Garrick, his lighting director (as well as graphic artist and designer of most of his later album jackets):

"It no longer was like [the appearance of] an entertaining troubadour, but more like a crusade, where sometimes I met people in the audience, women in their seventies who didn't come to the concert with their daughters or their sons, but came on their own to really receive the message . . . We did a show in Boston called Amandala with artistes like Dick Gregory and Patti Labelle, to collect funds for the Freedom Fighters in South Africa. That day, when Bob was into his encore, he really preached right through the songs. He made new lyrics on the spot. In fact [it is then that] one of the lines from 'Redemption Song' came to be."

Ironically Marley's performances at home in Jamaica had been rather intermittent. He once said, "I don't really bury my head in Jamaica, you know. I'm talking to the people over the world."

The Reggae King's first performance had been at the Queen's Theatre on Kes Chin's Talent Parade in Kingston, which won him the riches of a pound. This was followed by the Derrick Morgan Farewell Concerts in Montego Bay and May Pen in the beginning of the sixties and Clement Dodd's arena shows where he went over in a big way.

Bob Marley and Stevie Wonder jamming it together in Jamaic 1975 (above) an in 1979 at the Black Music Association meeting in Philadelphia (below).

There were notable performances by Marley with Marvin Gaye (1973), Jackson 5 (1974), and Stevie Wonder (1975), in which the Rastaman's vibrations left a lasting impression on the visitors. Then of course there were the memorable Smile Jamaica and One Love Peace Concerts in 1976 and 1978 respectively.

Bob Marley and the Wailers led the musical line-up for Reggae Sunsplash (1979) and in the same year performed charitably for International Year of the Rasta Child and the Ethiopian Orthodox Church's benefits.

After the 1980 European tour, Bob Marley produced his last album: *Uprising.* It was like a sequel to *Survival* in terms of its message content. The cry for revolution, the apocalyptic vision, were there—yet the tone was less war-like, more infused with almost intangible sadness. At points there were notes of disillusionment.

It's too late . . . men have lost their faith . . .
We no know how me and them a go
work this out

("We And Them")

Yet the positive vibes were there. "Coming In From The Cold", an assertion of victory over evil, reached the Top Five in Britain. And the final word in consolation and hope—though again this was tinged with sorrow—was the outstanding, powerful, immeasurably beautiful "Redemption Song". It was almost as if Marley knew that the day of his transition was near, and wanted to leave a legacy to his "bredren" and "sistren" of the world.

The band then crossed over to the United States. The Madison Square Garden sets which took

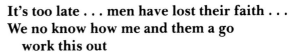

145

place in September 1980 had that variety fare which proved to be a friendly trap set to catch a share of audience that had never been caught before by reggae. The Black Market. Marley had courted his "special market" by appearing at Harlem's famed Apollo Theatre in the fall of 1979 doing an unprecedented four-day set. At the Madison Square Garden gig, Marley was joined by the Commodores, one of Motown's hottest properties, and the reigning rapper, Kurtis Blow, whose popular style is traceable to the "toasting" formula long practised in Jamaica and Africa before that. When the musical deeds were done, the general consensus was that the roof was taken off the Madison by the roots, rocking rhythm of reggae.

It was to serve as a prelude to what would have been billed as the concert of the century: Stevie Wonder and Bob Marley and the Wailers doing a no-holds-barred North American tour. The fact that this tour had to be cancelled after Marley fell ill must have been one of his greatest disappointments, since it was here that he planned to capture the black market once and for all.

Wonder, who openly expressed his brotherly and artistic love for Marley on many occasions, could easily find his own way on stage with Bob in earshot. They had first appeared together in Jamaica in 1975 (along with Roberta Flack) at the Dream Concert. In 1979 at the Black Music Association's meeting in Philadelphia, the forum primarily for black executives in the music industry, the delegates had gone into extended recess after hearing Wonder join the Rastaman who had earlier pleaded "play I on the R&B. . . ."

Bob performing at the 1979 Reggae Sunsplash in Montego Bay, Jamaica (top); Black Uhuru (centre), and Steel Pulse (bottom)—two contemporary reggae groups at the '81 Reggae Sunsplash.

146

Bob and The Commodores at Madison Square Garden, 1979 (left); and four internationally renowned performers who have been "clinging tight to the reggae vine": The Clash, The Police, Paul Simon and Barbra Streisand.

The visionary Wonder would later pay his personal respects and tribute to the King of Reggae at the 1981 Reggae Sunsplash music marathon held in Montego Bay. It could have been described as the "hello sunshine" concert as the beauty of the Jamaican sunrise peeped out over the mountain to shine on the children of Jah.

Musically, Stevie Wonder's improvisations and interpretations of reggae were lessons in taking the music past its limitless borders and beyond with Marley serving as the guiding light. Wonder's "Boogie On Reggae Woman", an early effort, had bridged musical waters. "Masterblaster" was Stevie's salute to Marley, a rendition of "Jamming", which was "Hotter Than July" on the jukeboxes and bulleted to the top of the international charts.

Marley was truly a masterblaster. He blasted reggae through previously impermeable cultural barriers. Because of his influence, other artistes besides Wonder, like the Beatles, the Rolling Stones, Paul Simon, Barbara Streisand, Roberta Flack and more recently the Police, the Specials, the Beat, Joe Jackson and the Clash, all began to cling tight to the reggae music vine.

RollingStone
Edizione Italiana

BOB MARLEY
Finalmente in Italia!

REPORTAGE
GABRIEL GARCIA MARQUEZ
Le guerre del Vietnam

Friday, December 7, 1979

Bob Marley shows anguish during concert at the University of Kansas
Mark Hinojosa/staff

Political Performer

Marley Moves Fans to Frenzy

Music in Mid-America

By Nancy Ball
Entertainment Editor

BOB MARLEY AND THE WAILERS in concert in Hoch Auditorium at the University of Kansas, Lawrence, Kan.: Bob Marley, lead vocals and guitar; with the Wailers, including Aston Barrett, bass; Carlton Barret, drums; Tyrone Downie and Earl Lindo, keyboards; Al Anderson and Donald Kerr, guitar; Alvin Patterson, percussion; Ms. Rita Marley and Ms. Judy Mowatt, background vocals. With PAT'S BLUE RIDDIM BAND, featuring Robert Zahn. Produced by NeoSpace and SUA.

It's been a long and frustrating wait for reggae fans in the Kansas City area, but the Jamaican star Bob Mar...

Marley's politics is grounded in the Bible. Based on Old Testament writings, Rastafarianism began with the slaves who were brought to Jamaica and teaches that the Africans of the world will one day unite to throw off oppression.

Most of its believers, like Marley, grow their hair into long, twisted plaits...

Nevertheless, Marley and company turned in a muscular set that included songs from the "Survival" LP such as "Wake Up and Live," "Ambush" and "Ride Natty Ride." There also were powerfully rendered Marley classics such as "No Woman No Cry," "Natty Dread," "Jamming," "Get Up, Stand Up," and "I Shot the Sheriff."

For Marley's set a large portrait of Haile Selasie, the late Emperor of Ethiopia, was unfurled in kingly robes, wrapped at the back of the stage like an enormous icon. The picture of Selasie...

PAGE 18...BIG RED...NOVEMBER 4, 1979

BOB MARLEY ROCKS THE APOLLO

STORY BY OSEYE MCHAWI/PHOTOS BY WAF

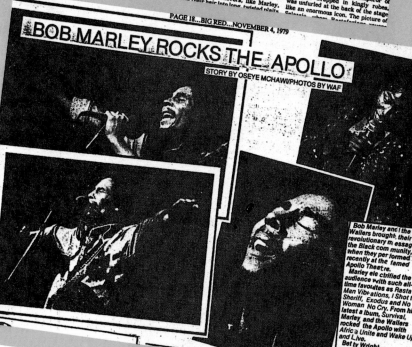

Bob Marley and the Wailers brought their revolutionary message to the Black community when they performed recently at the famed Apollo Theatre.

Marley electrified the audience with such all-time favorites as Rasta Man Vibrations, I Shot the Sheriff, Exodus and No Woman No Cry. From his latest album, Survival, Marley and the Wailers rocked the Apollo with Africa Unite and Wake Up and Live.

Betty Wright preceded Marley and the Wailers and gave a rousing performance.

> "His fans come for the music but it's the message they take away."
> (Jon Bradshaw, *L.A. Times*, Aug. 14, 1977)

BLACK ECHOES

November 25, 1978

15p

Page 10 BLACK ECHOES

November 25, 1978

BOB MARLEY — Rastaman, not Rock star

Interview by Alex Skorecki

"What a glorious morning, when we land in Liberia shore, and behold a time when black man shall weep no more. Behold this big moon just come right over your own land. And the big moon just climb right on top of the mountain. And the big moon nobody hustlin' you down, and in y'own land. And been said, let it be done, we are the children of the rastaman."

ROADSHOWS

Record Mirror, July 18, 1...

HYPNOTIC MARLEY

BOB MARLEY AND THE WAILERS
Apollo, Glasgow

ANCIENT RHYTHMIC tribal hypnotism — that's what it is. Bob Marley in the Caribbean gun sent to quarantine joy, love and personal fulfilment.

BOB MARLEY: come join the party

NEW SINGLE
DEEP PURPLE

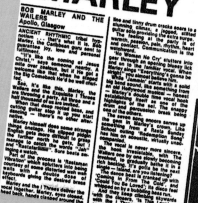

Le calvaire d'Hinault

Il a pris le départ de l'étape qui conduit le Tour à St-Malo

France-Soir

toute dernière

2 F

Rapt du P.-D.G. : Maintenant l'angoisse

P.T.T. : vers une menace de grève générale

Pas le moindre signe des ravisseurs depuis six jours

• Trois hypothèses

50.000 spectateurs pour Bob Marley...

... et trois gangsters qui volent la recette

Remaniement ministériel ?

Le petit

Le temps prévu samedi

Talens rigere oktav

En vindhas – eller deklamationskunstens Nestor?

IDA LINDENBORG

Fremragende Marley

MUSIK

BOB MARLEY & WAILERS

Kaalø skriver om et andet dukkehjem

SPØRG OM SPROGET

> *"When you smoke herb it reveals you to yourself. All the wickedness that you do is revealed by the herb—it's your conscience and it gives you an honest picture of yourself. Herb makes you meditate . . . it's only a natural thing and it grows like a tree."*
>
> (Speaking to Richard Cromelin, *Rolling Stone*)

ジャム

シティライフとロックが出会う音楽雑誌

El Correo Catalán

Martes, 1 de julio de 1980

La «barretina» de Marley

El cantante jamaicano Bob Marley actuó anoche en la plaza de toros Monumental de Barcelona. Por la tarde, compareció en el coso taurino para efectuar las pruebas de sonido, ataviado con una curiosa «barretina» multicolor. Esta variante de la tradicional prenda catalana, colocada en la testa de un antillano, fue motivo de singulares comentarios entre los empleados de la plaza. (Foto: Fausto).

Barcelona: Antoni Rubio, presidente del gremio de hoteleros

BARCELONA. — Antonio Rubio Garcés, que regenta también la presidencia de la Confederación Empresarial de Hostelería de Cataluña ha sido nombrado presidente del Gremio de Hoteles de Barcelona, durante la asamblea general extraordinaria que tuvo lugar ayer en el hotel Princesa Sofía.

En la misma reunión salió elegida la junta directiva por un periodo de tres años, quedando como vicepresidentes: Manuel González Gómez, Juan Gaspart Bonet y José Mestres Blanc; secretario: Javier Coromina Barba; José Bascompte Solá, como interventor y José María Vallés Marroc y Luis Tusquets Barrondo como vicesecretario y tesorero respectivamente.

Los cargos vocales recayeron sobre: Francisco Orobitg Lloreta, Joaquín Verdú Alois, José Ríos Sierra, Evaristo Moliné García, José María Callis Moliné, José María González Simó, Manuel Martí Risco, José Badía Almirall, José María Herrero Villanueva, Ricardo Domingo Monfort y Rafael Lleó Bernadó.

... Y más n

Los socialistas amenazan con otra moción de censura

MADRID. — Los socialistas podrían volver a plantear una nueva moción de censura contra el Gobierno si éste contiúa con su mala gestión, según declaró ayer x Logos Alfonso Guerra, tras la reunión que celebraron los grupos socialistas del Senado y el Congreso.

El PSC-PSOE presenta su segundo congreso

BARCELONA. — El segundo congreso del PSC-PSOE, que se celebrará durante el próximo fin de semana, fue presentado ayer. El congreso, que contará con la presencia de 395 delegados (representando a unos 25.000 militantes) será complejo, como la actual sociedad catalana, pero será el de la

---

CARIBBE'

P.O. Box 20546, Philadelphia, Pennsylvania, 19138
Volume 1, Number 4 November, 1979

Rastaman Rocks Penn Hall

When a concert audience goes to listen to the performers have played before in any case, you know something special is happening. At Bob Marley and the Wailers Penn Hall appearance last Wednesday, the audience stood on chairs as soon as Marley and the Wailers tapped on stage.

Marley waved their arms in the air and swayed as Marley reached a brief prayer to the Honor of His Father.

"Then the band kicked into its opening chords of "Rastaman Vibration," playing so deliberately and earnestly that the confidence of their faith flowed out from the stage and embraced the audience. The Wailers' steady rock spoke it clear that they felt so much in chords the people with flesh — in spite of all of Babylon's glitter they would play deep and strong from their hearts.

Under a banner bearing the image of the Emperor, Haile Selassie, Marley led the band into a audience-shy chant. "We are African people, We are African people." The thundering bass seemed to be echoing from the sky and a saxophone pierced as to echo to Marley's cry. The chant turned the more then 4,000 people in the hall into an instant community. Even as Philadelphia's Mayor-elect promised to bring people together, the Wailers brought together young and old, black and white in dancing unity.

Those who stood on chairs, roamed around the hall, straining for a glimpse of Bob, dancing, talking, yelling and shaking wooden rattles being sold around the hall. Previous girls pressed around the auditorium pillars as old friends greeted each other with warm smiles and open arms. Long-hairs hung off comfortably on blankets by the walls, nodding blissfully. No one seemed to mind when their view of the stage was blocked; being a part of the celebration seemed to be just as satisfying as seeing the show.

Those who could see the stage were galvanized when Jr. Marvin stepped out front for a whining guitar solo on "Dread Locks Dread" that sent him reeling onto his back, sparking screams from the audience. That first high point blended with a loose, relaxed percussion jam as the Wailers dished up "Ambush" from the new Survival LP, which may be the hardest Marley LP ever.

The concert began to shift gears with "War," a spotlight hitting the face of the Emperor as Marley recited Selassie's words, taken from his epic United Nations address. After a dark "Africa Unite," things picked up again when Marley put down his guitar, closed his eyes and began to sing "One Drop." "I know Jah would never let us down, pull your rights from wrong...it dread, it dread, dread, dread!" As he chanted "dread" over and over, he rubbed his dreadlocks, bringing another cheer from the crowd. Then he danced himself into ecstasy, prancing away from the microphone and back, to the Wailers vamping on "Ride Natty Ride," taking him back to Africa.

The I-Threes, whose backing vocals had risen above the rhythm throughout, began to dance off-stage, followed by Marley. The stage went dark; the music stopped. A sudden explosion of cheering and clapping came from the throng. Mfind down the ground on their chairs. The roar grew more insistent, continuing for nearly five minutes until the stage lights came up and the Wailers

Inside Caribbe'

Top Ranking	3
More Marley	4
Reggae Review	5
Arts and Entertainment	6
Buy It Local	7
Editorial	8
Polemix	9
Reggae	10
Afrobeat	10
Positive Outlook	11
Sugar Sunday	11

"A stranger would have thought it was a political rally or a religious revival, not a pop concert. Bob Marley's vision of revelation and revolution may not ever come to pass, but if it does, it will be an apocalypse you can dance to."

(Larry Rohter, *Washington Post*, April 26, 1976)

"Ancient rhythmic tribal hypnotism"
(*Record Mirror*)

Ingen navn er Bob Marley og Irvis du ikke kender ham, kommer du til det...

HANS MUSIK ER SÅ STÆRK AT HAN TVINGER DIG TIL AT LYTTE!

On the peace concert:

"... Since reggae in general and Marley in particular hold tremendous sway over the island [Jamaica], he was pushed into the center of the storm.
"In his music, he has always been able to combine a primitive, roots feeling with such pop niceties as melody and good lyric hooks, but that's not the real reason he's a star. He is also a galvanizing performer with a flair for drama ... His serious statements are sometimes mistaken for put-ons; his put-ons sometimes get taken seriously. Alone among reggae stars, Bob Marley has an Image."

(John Morthland, *Newsday*, March 26, 1978)

PAULEY PAVILION CONCERT

Marley Sends His Message Through Special Delivery

BY ROBERT HILBURN
Times Pop Music Critic

You don't usually get a second chance at superstardom in rock, but Bob Marley may just pull it off.

The Jamaican reggae singer was one of the few bold, uplifting figures in rock in the mid-1970s when the scene was so uninspired that many fans understandably asked, "Where have all the heroes gone?"

Despite the charisma and his music's social comment that led to comparison with Mick Jagger and Bob Dylan, Marley never quite reached the predicted stardom in this country. His "Rastaman Vibration" album made the Top 10 in 1976, but a foot ailment, which forced the cancellation of a crucial tour, and disappointing product prevented him from cementing the popularity.

Just when he seemed to be fading from sight, however, Marley has bounced back with his most forceful album in years. Ironically, it's titled "Survival" and it bristles with the songwriter's anti-oppression doctrine.

The question Friday night at UCLA's Pauley Pavilion was whether Marley, 34, could still deliver live.

An advantage the small crop of passionate artists had in the mid-1970s was that they had little competition. With passion and energy no longer novel, such one-time standouts as Suzi Quatro and, to a lesser extent, David Johansen have lost some of their original lure.

Marley needn't worry about the new-wave forces, many of whom (including the Police and Clash) have been influenced by him. In his first local appearance in nearly 18 months, Marley remains one of the most commanding figures in all of pop.

Marley's highly sensual music, now accented by two horn players, is perhaps the most physical on the contemporary scene: slashing guitar licks, whistle drumbeats, stabbing organ notes and a bass line so potent that it virtually vibrates through your body.

By the end of the evening, the Pauley Please Turn to Page 8, Col. 3

SPREADING THE WORD—Jamaica's Bob Marley combines music and Rastafarian religious doctrine in concert at UCLA's

BOB MARLEY VIEWS A RELIGIOUS PATH CALLED RASTAFARI AS THE HOPE OF THE WO...
... It looks upon Ethiopia's late emperor Haile Selassie, right, as a god

Zürichs Reggae-Fans feierten Bob Marley

Friday, November 2, 1979 ● ● ●

High-lights

DAVID BROMBERG TO PLAY TONIGHT
... he will be presented by the Lane Series

Bromberg in Concert

David Bromberg Band performing in concert today at 8 p.m. in Memorial Auditorium. A musician impossible to classify, Bromberg is a part of everything that is contemporary music. He and his band will offer Vermont fans a smorgasbord of sounds in the great tradition of Bromberg. Also appearing will be Kilimanjaro. Tickets are priced at $8.25, $6.75 and $4.75.

First Aid for Sagging Homes

Bob Marley Tells of Being a Rastaman

By SUSAN GREEN
Free Press Staff Writer

> "The fundamental elements of his philosophy were the self redemption of the black race and the return of that race to the African continent to restore it to its ancient glory."
>
> (Tracy Nicholas,
> *Rastafari: A Way of Life*)

Bob Marley trygt på reggae-tronen

Innbruddstyv og romantiker med anfektelser

Bob Marley forsvandt Drammenshallen til en bek.segrise. (Foto: Kåre Eide)

—Vi er en familie, tross alt

SPETTACOLI

AFFLUENZA RECORD PER IL CANTANTE GIAMAICANO A SAN SIRO, TRASFORMATO PER UNA SERA IN UNA «WOODSTOCK» ITALIANA

Centomila allo stadio: Bob Marley batte gli «europei»

Giovani di tante città, tutti insieme, per ballare il «reggae»

Bob Marley: il «sentore» ieri ha vinto a San Siro

Giuseppina Manin

GRUPPO CHIMICO IMPORTANZA MONDIALE

per il potenziamento del proprio Servizio Elaborazione Dati dotato di un sistema IBM 370/148 (DOS/VS - CICS - DL/1) ricerca:

A) **Analista-programmatore**
cui affidare la responsabilità di importanti procedure, in particolare quelle relative alla Gestione del Personale.

Titoli richiesti:
— esperienza almeno triennale nell'area applicativa suddetta, conoscenza dei linguaggi COBOL, istruttiva alla conoscenza di collaboratori; conoscenza di alcune materie superiori, di età 28/35 anni.

Titoli preferenziali:
— conoscenza linguaggio ASSEMBLER e CICS.

B) **Programmatore esperto**

C'erano anche i soliti «portoghesi» (pochi)

Setting standard Jam album reviewe

JAMAICAN LION INNA CONCRETE JUNGLE
Bob Marley in Harlem
By NEIL SPENCER

> "... He was, above all else, a symbol of hope and optimism for millions of fellow humans around the world, who saw in the diminutive singer from Trenchtown some aspect of their own sufferings or torments, some resilience and militancy that they lacked or aspired to ..."
>
> (Neil Spencer, *New Musical Express*,
> May 16, 1981)

ECHOES

MARLEY MATTERS

"*I motored down through Babylon by bu with Bob and his band whic allowed a first hand look at the group. There is a pervasive good humoured bantering among them, and they are a surprisingly healthy lot by rock standards.*"

(Roger Steffen L.A. Weekl

"*Marley's exceptional show generated the kind of intense emotional celebration—some called that kind of experience 'magic'—that results when a performer not only meets the high expectancy level but actually gives his audience new reasons to believe . . .*"

(L.A. Times)

Marley wails up a storm

By CHRISTINE CAMP

● BOB MARLEY . . . wailing at Festival Hall last night.

Call for Lib 'bribe' probe

By ALLISON BROUWER

THE Australian Democrats have called for a public inquiry into what they say are bribe attempts by Liberal candidates or supporters over preference allocation at the May 5 state election.

Bob Marley

Jamaican Musician Denounces Racism and Violence

Susan Green

There couldn't have been a more poignant soundtrack to the North Carolina massacre, still fresh in my mind thanks to graphic television footage of the murderous rampage on an Klan rally, than several of Bob Marley's...

BOB MARLEY SINGS AT BURLINGTON CONCERT
. . . he's clowned at the 'way earthly things are going'

"*At Madison Square Garden last September, referring to the first of those concerts Robert Palmer of the New York Times wrote of its 'mesmerizing atmosphere' and of Mr. Marley's spellbinding performance and 'intense singing and electric stage presence.'*

"*With its link to the Rastafarian religious movement of Jamaica, reggae had a messianic political message that lifted it beyond the simpler pleasantries of ordinary popular music, and Mr. Marley more than anyone conveyed and embodied that message.*"

(John Rockwell, New York Times, Dec. 5, 1981)

FOR THE LARGEST
OF TOYS SEE
MAURA'S
BIG TOYLAND
OPEN DAILY UNTIL

Ministe
speaks
educati
standar

EDUCATION M
Derrell Rolle declared
House of Assembly las
that every level of educ
the Bahamas must be s
establish and account
own standard,
ANTHONY FORBES

The Minister also said
courses in Maths and Eng
ordinary and remedial
must be compulsory fo
Bahamas is to obtain a
standard of education
secondary level.

Speaking during the
budget debate, Mr Rolle
that the time has come w
responsible people must
stock of our education sy
and see where we are goin

He said that Bahamians
now focus their attention
the quality of education a
offered in our system. It
be designed for the needs
interest of our country,
said.

Mr Rolle also said that
must strive to develop a
regard for competence

THOUSANDS of
Bahamians and photo-snap-
ping tourists lined Nassau and
Bay Streets, Kemp and Wulff
Roads today as Jamaican
reggae superstar Bob Marley
and the Wailers hit town.

Mr Marley arrived on a

Bahamasair flight from
Florida shortly after 10:30
am this morning and was
welcomed by Mrs Beryl
Hanna, chairperson of the
national commission of the
International Year of the
Child, Mrs Rubie Nottage,
head of the fund-raising

committee, and Miss Telenna
Coakley, secretary, in the
airport's VIP lounge.

The national commission is
sponsoring the benefit
concert scheduled for
tomorrow night at the Queen
Elizabeth Sports Centre in

which Mr Marley will appear
along with American singer
Betty Wright.

Mr Marley (centre) is
caught here by photographer
Derek Smith along with two
members of his band during
the motorcade through New
Providence after his arrival.

THE REGGAE WAY TO 'SALVATION'

Out of Jamaica comes a star singing hellfire, revolution and biblical beginnings. To the
'downpressed' of the third world, Bob Marley is a hero. Now he takes on America.

By Jon Bradshaw

So he comes jiggling out onto the
stage, this wiry, spindle-shanked
singer, this self-styled black prince
of reggae, his clenched fist high
above his head, his dreadlocks flop-
ping round his ears. The crowd rises
to its feet and begins to scream and
the singer shouts, "Yes!" and the
crowd shouts, "Yes! Yes!" And then, with
slight menace in his voice, the singer says, "Jeo-,
begins fire to my salvation. Whom shall I fear?
Jah, Ras Tafari," And the crowd screams, "Jah,
Jah, Ras Tafari" and begins to whistle and clap and

the band begins to play and the singer slides into one
of his early songs called "Lively Up Yourself."

It is the final concert of Bob Marley and the Wailers' European tour at the Rainbow Theater in
London. His American tour begins next Thursday at
New York City's Palladium. After six albums in the
last five years, Bob Marley has emerged as Jamaica's chief cultural hero, its Cassandra, singing won-
derfully well of doom and desolation. Despite the
growing popularity of reggae (pronounced REG-
gay) music, it is most odd that this Caribbean wild
man, with his dreadlocks, his ganja-inspired revelations, has attracted such a hysterical following. A
gospel of death to the "downpressors" does not seem
in keeping with these fame times.

But here he is in front of an overcrowded house,
half of them black, half of them white, singing of
burning and boxing, of revolution, of lightning, thunder, brimstone and fire. On the stage behind Marley
is a lurid backdrop, complete with huts, fires and
telegraph poles — meant to resemble Trenchtown,
the squalid Kingston ghetto where he was raised. To
the right of the stage is the flag of Ethiopia and a
banner depicting the Conquering Lion of Judah. At
Marley's previous London concert, there were
numerous stabbings and tonight the police and vigi-

*Jon Bradshaw is a contributing editor of Esquire
and is currently writing a novel about the black revolution in Rhodesia.*

VOICE

BOB MARLE
SATISFIES
HIS SOUL

REILS(P-3)

Marley's music picks up a gloss

By ...

Entertainment

SPOTLIGHTS

Mork sues
for $5 million

LOS ANGELES —

Foxx's wife says he hit her

Stratford trio honored

What's on tonight

> "We're
> oppressed, so
> we sing
> oppressed
> songs and
> sometimes
> people find
> themselves
> guilty."
> (Marley)
> (Jon Bradshaw,
> *New York
> Times*, Aug. 14,
> 1977)

Reggae returns
Bob Marley and the Wailers prove it's still a strapping sound

...ck/Rick Kogan

Though it says so above, it wasn't rock that
Bob Marley and the Wailers played Tuesday
night at the Uptown. It was reggae, and for a
musical form many predicted was dead or
as soon about to be, it certainly proved to
a lively and strapping sound that formed
...e of the fall's finest concerts.

But there was some apprehension before the
...ow. Although Marley was said to have fully
...covered from the shooting incident a few
...ears ago in Jamaica, his last few albums
...ounded suspiciously flat and lifeless. And
...ven as the evening's show began, Marley and
the Wailers seemed wanting for some energy.

It wasn't long, however, before Marley was
...ancing a Jamaican jig to "I Shot the Sheriff"
...his most famous song) and the audience was
...esponding enthusiastically, their fears al-
...ayed.

THOUGH THE CURRENT group of Wailers
(10 men and two women vocalists) is vastly
inferior to previous editions, Marley has never
...een better, commanding the stage with exce-
...handed authority and visual sparks. (His dred-
...locks looked almost otherworldly.)

His impassioned vocals—and it is important
to note that Marley isn't singing about lying
on the beach, he is singing songs of black survival and political strife—were gentler than
in former years. He was just the ...

**His impassioned vocals—
and it is important to note
that Bob Marley isn't
singing about lying on the
beach, he is singing songs
of black survival and
political strife—were
gentler than in former years.**

ingly alike after a while, that was not, and
has never really been, Marley's problem. Each
number was well-defined, building to an as-
tounding blast of an encore, highlighted by
"Get Up, Stand Up."

IN FACT, it is difficult to think of any
problems Tuesday night. It is, therefore, time
to consider the reasons why reggae, once
...he next big rock craze, never rap-

But this infectious music never did explode
on the public, never did ... the appeal to
capture mass audiences. Those of the Uptown
could have cared less. They were moving and
shouting and loving every ... of the ...
...thing called reggae and why not?

When Bob Marley and the Wailers played,
there was no time for questions. There was
...ony and dancing and hardly enough time at

ASTON "FAMEY MAN" BARRETT

CARLTON BARRETT

ALVIN "SECCO" PATTERSON

TYRONE "ORGAN D" DOWNIE

MW
M...
...JAM...

ボブ・マーリィ&ザ・ウエイラーズ日本ツアー

ようこそ！ ...

5th to 13th, April, Tokyo & Osaka, JAPAN

THE WAILERS

Melody Maker

August 11, 1979   10p weekly   USA: one dollar

BOB MARLEY: UPTOWN GHETTO LIVING

Interview by VIVIEN GOLDMAN (p. 24)

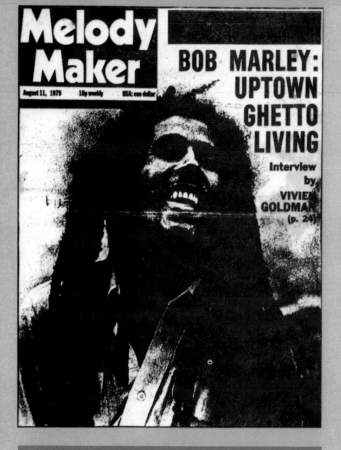

> "We're not talking about burnin' and lootin' for material goods. We want to burn capitalistic illusions."
>
> (Bob Marley)

ISTHMUS
OF MADISON

Vol. 4, No. 42   Nov. 9-15, 1979

Music

Reggae Down To The Roots

We've seen reggae garner a growing audience among rock, jazz and folk music fans in America, but Jamaica's musical style has yet to break through into the mainstream of soul and disco enthusiasts. The Third World band, who've dispensed some truly noteworthy reggae, have sadly chosen to ped some of their albums with outright thumpa-thumpa-thumpa American-style disco tunes to achieve this end. We've even heard this sort of behavior from Jacob Miller and Peter Tosh, two of the dreadest fellows this side of Port Royal. It's disappointing, because the blatant beat of disco manages, usually, to cloud the delicate syncopations of good reggae: the two mix like oil and water.

Bob Marley and the Wailers have released an album that, with the right promotion, could break through that barrier—and you won't find a thumpa-thumpa-thumpa disco tune on the disc. The tones on Survival (Island Records [LPS 9542]) have a rhythm and a slick production feel that could win over even the farthest-gone disco freak, yet there's a genuine roots sensibility that penetrates most of the cuts.

Some of the most interesting selections, musically, are "Africa Unite" and "Ambush in the Night," which features some nice clarinet punctuation on the chorus. Check also "One Drop," with its vintage rock R&B chord progression and arrangement. "Wake Up and Live" typifies the engrossing, hypnotic spell that marks much reggae, and features a sax solo—doubly interesting because reggae isn't a solo-oriented music.

The lyrics are no... as well, with Marley's usual optimist/revolutionary viewpoints pervading the album. The words will sting at one moment of the oppression of Third World peoples, but the next moment always returns to the happy world that will result from united effort against the oppressors.

The entire album carries special messages to the African ethos (Rasta idiom for children). From the concept of:

> "How good and pleasant it would be, before God and man...
> To see the unification of all Africans: As it's been said already, let it be done right now:
> We are the children of the Rastaman."
>
> ("Africa Unite" ©1979, Bob Marley Music, Ltd.)

to the specific suggestion:

> "Natty dread it ina Zimbabwe; Set it up ina Zimbabwe; Mash it up ina Zimbabwe; Africans a liberate Zimbabwe."
>
> ("Zimbabwe" ©1979, Bob Marley Music, Ltd.)

Marley's lead vocals and rhythm guitar work are backed by the always dependable Barretts on bass, drums and other instruments. The musicians are some of Jamaica's greatest, including Rita Marley, Judy Mowatt and Marcia Griffiths, the wonderful I Threes vocal group. The whole project was recorded and mixed at Marley's own Tuff Gong studio in Kingston, which has a clean, tight sound compared to the run-of-the-mill, back-room Jamaican studio. While there's no way to know yet if the entire run is to be blessed, the pressing I heard was smooth and quiet.

I mon self, "Check it" And if this sort of groove sounds good to you, drop by the Coliseum next Sunday night, when Marley and the Wailers will be thanking live on stage. Go deh!

—Rick Murphy

> Neville: *Could we talk a little bit about how you started out in this singing business? I know you started very young. How did you start?*
>
> Bob: *Started out crying.*

> "Our music is there to deal with the conditions where we come from. The music is like the news. The music influence the people. The music do everything for the people; the music tell the people what to do in Jamaica...."
>
> (To Stephen Davis, *Black Music & Jazz Review*)

AZ münchen

Montag, 2. Juni 1980   Seite 26

Die Haare gerieten in Elektro-Quirl: Kind skalpiert

30 000 beim Rock-Spektakel im Reitstadion

Open-Air-Festival mit vielen berühmten Gruppen

Von Thomas Vaseniis

Bob Marley kam - mit ihm die Stimmung

> "His songs have a hypnotic seductiveness... smooth inexorability... the cumulative sweep of the similar sounding songs amounts to a highly convincing stylistic attribute rather than a limitation. In any case the great Marley songs, like 'No Woman, No Cry,' raise themselves out of the general welter like sentinels."
>
> (John Rockwell, *New York Times*, May 2, 1976)

Albums

Standing room only

BOB MARLEY & THE WAILERS: 'Babylon By Bus' (Island ISLD 11)

'Positive Vibration'; 'Punky Reggae Party'; 'Exodus'; 'Stir It Up'; 'Rat Race'; 'Concrete Jungle'; 'Kinky Reggae'; 'Lively Up Yourself'; 'Rebel Music'; 'War'; 'No More Trouble'; 'Is This Love'; 'Heathen'; 'Jamming'.

I can still hear three thousand people in the Hammersmith Odeon swaying in unison and chanting "everything's gonna be alright." This was the defiant optimism that swept Bob Marley from the deprivation of Trenchtown to the massive auditoriums of the '78 world tour.

Two years later 'No Yourself' from the 'Natty Woman No Cry' (the live Dread album still remain...

committed to record. Since then he has explored rhythms linked to Exodus and featured with sensitive love songs reference 'Kaya.' But never has he equalled the strength and youthful confidence he achieved on the first live album.

Bob Marley is no longer the musician cum poet / prophet (sic). He may have been the first on Radio 1 to chant the Rasta message when he was stranded in the Kingston Concrete Jungle. Now he is public property. He has a responsibility to his new audience and his record company.

BOB MARLEY

knows it's there and can't figure out how to plug it.

He struck the ice-berg 'Kaya' and has now packed it out with 'Babylon By Bus' wedding. This is a double album recorded at unspecified venues in Paris, Copenhagen, London and Amsterdam...

sleeves are replaced. They're all here. All of his best songs 'Exodus' 'Jamming' and 'Punky Reggae Party.' Our leader praises and cries throughout probably trying to drag some enthusiasm out of his backing singers. The I Threes...

Bathylon By Bus is a good live album. It serves as a seasonal package to keep the kids at bay for a few more months, while Bob figures out his next move.

—Jon Futrell

TINA CHARLES: 'Greatest Hits' (CBS 83201)

'I Love To Love (But My Baby Loves To Dance)'; 'Dance Little Lady Dance'; 'Rendezvous'; 'It's Here I Come A Change (of Heart)'; 'Hold Me'; 'You Set My Heart On Fire'; 'Dr Love'; 'I'll Go Where Your Music Takes Me'; 'My Lover's Song'; 'Bounce, For My Sweet'; 'Love Me Like A...

Lover; 'Makin' All Those Moves'

The little Lady bounces in with a palpitation of her greatest, all comfortably by Mr UK Disco Biddu. The focus on dancing, and the outstanding track first ever "hit" My Heart On Fire of course by Biddu fortunately backs "boom shboom" back the single.

Most of the tracks are well known around played Disco hits past couple of years from the same more few slower ones 'Hold Me' fall nice place to punctuate faster rhythms.

But sadly, it's nitely Discomusic past.

—Ara

> "Reggae is created by people who have known suffering, who are disenfranchised, torn from their past and yet whose music is constantly redeemed by hope."
>
> (Roger Steffens, *L.A. Weekly*, Nov. 30, 1979)

The Nassau Guardian

YEAR 136 - VOL. 21   NASSAU, BAHAMAS, MONDAY, DECEMBER 17, 1979   36 PAGES   15 CENTS

B eatery et to take trike vote

Defence Force apprehends 19 for poaching

By EDWIN LIGHTBOURN

Nineteen foreigners apprehended by Defence Force personnel over the weekend, are expected to appear in the magistrate's court early this week to face charges of poaching in Bahamian waters and unlawful possession of marijuana and firearms.

The men, believed to be Cuban-Americans, include the captains and crewmen of the foreign vessels ranging from 35 to 46 feet.

Two of the fishermen were reportedly injured when one of the foreign vessels tried to ram the 'Marlin', one of the two Defence Force vessels which made the arrest early Friday morning. The other vessel crash landed when the...

KINKY REGGAE — Rastaman Bob Marley and his Wailers and Betty Wright with her back-up band "Eternity" staged a benefit performance Saturday night at the QE Sports Centre on behalf of the Bahamas International Fine for Children. (A mini LIM attended the concert which is believed to have taken in something like $30,000. Above is a super-impacked of Wright, left and Marley as they go through their separate performances.

—Photo by BRUCE DELANEY

Opposition deplores ...ack on Vanguard

Commercial banks 'against...

L.A. WEEKLY

Free

The Publication of News, People, Entertainment, Art and Imagination in Los Angeles

November 30-December 6, 1979   Volume 1, Number 52

ROLLING STONE, DECEMBER 28, 1978-JANUARY 11, 1979

RECORDS

Reinvented reggae

Bob Marley: all you need is love

Babylon by Bus
Bob Marley and
the Wailers
Island

By Timothy White

JAMAICANS have a marvelously vivid word – *blue-swee* – to describe those who are wily and hard to pin down: i.e., the Bob Marleys of the world. In native folklore, these qualities of cunning are personified by Anancy, a legendary figure whose name comes from the Twi *ananse*, meaning spider. The Anancy stories, derived from the Ashanti and brought to Jamaica in the 1600s on slave ships from the Gold

ILLUSTRATION BY AL MILGROM

Music

Bob Marley's Dread Crusade

by Roger Steffens

At a critical crossroads for reggae music, Bob Marley has returned to the militant roots of protest and social consciousness that first brought him fame. Thus, it saddens me that his concerts last weekend in L.A. and San Diego were not sellouts. Undeniably a world-wide superstar, Marley was unable to fill U.C.L.A.'s Pauley Pavilion or San Diego's Sports Arena. The reason isn't quite clear, but it poses a crucial question. Is reggae music at a dead end, as the English quasi-reggae group, The Police, claimed last week during a sometimes arrogant press conference at A&M's L.A. headquarters? Or is it that the people just don't want to listen?

It seems ironic that a dreadlocked Jamaican should be writing the political anthems we Americans take with us into the Weighty '80s. Dylan's all blissed out on a joyless Jesus trip, and Marley is the obvious heir of his poet-a-commentator mantle. What people like the shrewd calculators behind The Police, and others of their synthesizing ilk, miss about reggae is this: it is, at base, message music. Not the inoffensive "message in a bottle" music of The Police's recent publicity campaign, but a bible-wielding, hellfire-and-damnation-for-the-wicked music closer, always, to spirituals than rock 'n' roll. You can't just cop a heavy bass riff and transform yourself into a reggae band. With few exceptions, reggae is created by people who have known suffering, who are disenfranchised, torn from their past, and yet whose music is constantly redeemed by hope. Reggae is the exact opposite of punk nihilism.

Jah Warriors

Central to an understanding of reggae music is the Rasta's unshakable belief in

Bob Marley, liquids tucked into a locks cap, commenting thru Babylon

Pauley venue. From our seats in the Concourse (more like the "flies") we were unable to make out any of Marley's spoken words whatsoever. And I, who have listened to Marley's music daily for seven years, had great trouble recognizing familiar songs. At the far end of the Concourse, the sound achieved a murky kind of clarity, but the place should obviously never be booked for musical acts.

I doubt, too, that I shall ever return there to bear the indignity of Avalon Attractions' "crowd control." Last year, at

A Bloodclot Mess

Not that Betty Wright's disco medley was any more worth seeing than the Imperials were last year at Burbank. In fact,

Marley's Burbank concert, Avalon provided one entrance to allow untold thousands of listeners into the Starlight Amphitheatre. This year, something similar happened at Pauley. On both occasions, huge numbers of people were trapped outside and missed the opening act.

the Wailers have never had an appropriate opening act. They should either dispense with one completely — Marley is certainly capable of carrying the show on his own — or help some of their less fortunate brethren in Jamaica gain some American exposure. Or why not give the opening spot to Marley's extraordinary backing vocal trio, the I Threes (who were the I Twos on this occasion, thanks to Marcia Griffiths' pregnancy). Relegating Marcia, Rita Marley and Judy Mowatt to a background role is like having Diana Ross, Barbra Streisand and Joni Mitchell along just for the shoop-shoops: an unconscionable waste.

Lest I seem unreasonably sour, let me hasten to add that Marley's San Diego date was quite another matter. I motored down through Babylon by bus with Bob and his band, which allowed a first-hand look at the group. There is a pervasive good-humored bantering among them, and they are a surprisingly healthy lot by rock standards. Although they consume a fair amount of herb ("The guys who cleaned the bus last time took home a half pound of roaches," the bus driver told me) there is little incoherence. Mysteriousness, yes, even evasiveness. But when they want you to be clear on a point, they'll glare intently and reason with you until the light of recognition leaps back from your eyes.

The San Diego show was a feast of roots dub, and Marley laid waste Stewart Copeland's assertion that roots reggae is incapable of growth and change. (At the press conference I mentioned earlier, Copeland justified The Police's adaptation of the reggae heritage by claiming that Jamaican musicians are "very conservative," and unwilling to experiment as his band does.) The "rockers" sound is the latest form of Jamaican experimentation, and Marley used it brilliantly in San Diego. Ace sound engineer Karl Pitterson gave exciting new "rockers" mixes to such old favorites as "Kinky Reggae," taking up as much as 80 percent of the mix with thundering bass lines and percussion crashing like the slam of bars on death row.

Steffens hosts "The Reggae Beat," L.A.'s only reggae radio show, on KCRW, FM.

Photo by Roger Steffens

WESTINDIAN WORLD

BOB MARLEY REVELATIONS FROM A WARRIOR

"When you ask them about Reggae they say Bob Marley sings the rebel music, but that's what people want to hear. What the raas-claat are they singing about 'Baby I love you' every-day for, Baby knows we love her."

(Speaking to Carl Gayle, *Black Music & Jazz Review*)

MARLE POWER

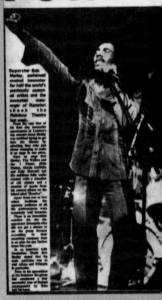

Bob Marley — reggaemusiker og Rastaprofet

Arts and Entertainment

Bob Marley breezes through the Apple with the Kingdom of Jah on his mind

By DON ROJAS

He is dubbed reggae's shining prince, a genuine superstar of contemporary music, modern Rasta prophet, revolutionary artist, visionary. Indeed, superlatives come easy when speaking of Robert Nesta Marley, 33, better known to millions as Bob Marley of the Wailers.

Much has been written about the "deeper" meanings of his music and about his exotic public persona but, as is the case with most exceptional talents, the attendant hype, the fantasies, fictions and distortions often vulgarize the reality of the artist as flesh and blood person with a distinct self-image.

Therefore, when one is given the rare opportunity to probe the man's more personal and intimate dimensions it's a chance a long-time admirer would hardly pass up. So armed with tape recorder and bubbling with ill-concealed excitement we leave the familiar, unpretentious turf of Central Brooklyn and make towards chic Central Park South in Manhattan.

It's one of those raw, forbidding days when to be outdoors is a test for anyone's resiliency. However, we find Marley (to whom cold weather is anathema) warmly ensconced in a plush suite in the Essex Towers Hotel. Only a cursory observation is enough to indicate that the Essex Towers is a favored watering hole for New York's power brokers who are not exactly in sync with a "dread" philosophy or a Rasta cosmology.

Does Marley feel out of place here? No. He claims to conquer his environment no matter how alien it is. This capitalistic ambience does not faze him. The almighty power of Jah is infinitely greater than the power of money.

As he speaks he exudes a tranquility that reflects extreme self confidence — an assurance that's nurtured partly by the realization of world-wide esteem and partly by having his inner circle of followers constantly defer to his wishes and point of view.

Dressed in skin-tight brown leather pants, pink jersey and green track shoes Marley speaks calmly but earnestly about the importance of the April 21 "peace...

BOB MARLEY

On himself as a stage performer:
Marley — Me no perform. Me love do things right. But me no love feel like me on a stage. I would love to break down a performance to a backyard situation. I would love to just talk with the brethren, reason with dem while entertaining. It must be an easy situation where everybody just relax up themselves and chat.

References to the attempt on his life; reactions to his critics and detractors:
Marley — 'Dem can't get me out so easy, man. Dem have to try harder than dat. Dem say me is a traitor to my people. No. No. No matter what propaganda dem spread about me I remain true to the masses. No man can change dat. Even if the masses say, 'Bob you not go on right', I remain true to the masses. Dat is my pay . . . to remain true. If I want get pay all me have to do is tell de truth."

On his Pan-African vision:
Marley — "Me just want Black consciousness to unite all Black people because the white man sitting alright; he have Europe, but Africa ain't built up yet because there is no unity. The time is right for unity. All dem liberation movements in Africa show dat all dem brethren get conscious now. Black man must come to know who his majesty Jah Rastafari is. Dat is the sweetest ting dat could happen to Black people. When the Black man trace his roots to Solomon and David he must move forward, all yuh belly move. Yuh no see?"

On his alleged involvement with race horse racketeering in Jamaica:
Marley — "Me no gamble you know Rasta. Man in Jamaica say me a win race horse. Me? I-man is a saint. My only vice is plenty woman. Other than dat I-man is a saint to all those accusations. His majesty give me a vision one time and say to me, 'don't gamble and don't involve yourself in a race horse business.' God, his majesty, is always right here wid me. I born wid a purpose. So when I talk about his majesty Jah Rastafari I am living proof. I defend Rastafari. See how dem beat down Rasta. No work, Divide and rule. Pressure people to bow down to Babylon. But dem can't mek me bow. Me conquer Babylon and all...

VIRUS MONTREAL

EN AVANT DE SON TEMPS

NOV 79   **$1.50**

LE GUI...

FILMS
THEATRE
RADIO
TELEVISION
RESTAURANTS

DANSE   MUSIQUE

ET PLUS...

> "His life ws a vital investment in the spiritual, emotional and intellectual energy badly needed by a people long engaged in that desperate search for self and purpose."
>
> (Basil Walters, *Jamaica Daily News*)

Bob Marley Rocks The Harlem Apollo!

Written & Photographed By Coreen Simpson

Jimmy Cliff

Chuck Jackson

Mr. Marley's lighting men was danci... alongside the controls and just hav... a wonderful time. After a really h... show, enjoyed tremendously by t... overflow crowd, Mr. Marley broug... two unique young men who da... with such zest and style that... audience came to its feet.

After the show I met Jimmy Cl... The Harder They Come fame.... Jackson took Jimmy and his... back to The St. Moritz Hotel.... rode in his limo Jimmy Cliff... and shyly spoke of his admir... Bob Marley. "Tomorrow I am... way to England...I have some... business there."

For those who missed Mr. M... time around remember next... get your ticket!!!

> "He audaciously used his immense talent to carry the message of the rights of the downtrodden and exploited into the chambers of the rich and the powerful."
>
> (Jamaica Council for Human Rights)

> ". . . he was a man with deep religious and political sentiments who rose from destitution to become one of the most influential music figures in the last twenty years."
>
> (Roger Steffens, *L.A. Weekly*, Nov. 30, 1979)

The Daily Gleaner

Vol. CXLVIII No. 53   ESTABLISHED 1834   KINGSTON, JAMAICA, MONDAY, FEBRUARY 8, 1982   SIXTEEN PAGES

60 CENTS

This is I Country

'RECOGNISE RASTAFARIANISM' — U.K. ROMAN CATHOLICS SAY

(From The Times)

LONDON
A PLEA for Rastafarianism to be recognised as a valid religion and for Rastafarians to be allowed to enjoy full religious rights has been made by the Roman Catholic Church in England and Wales.

However, the GLEANER had already published, on Saturday, the Government's decision to liberalise imports which was communicated by the Minister to the manufacturing sector at a meeting on Thursday.

...tio also urges that the Rastarian style of dress, including the characteristic "dreadlock" hairstyle, should be accepted by society as "authentic religious expressions and legitimate cults of forms".

The Home Office in particular is asked to observe these principles, and a copy of the document is...

...being set to the Home Secretary by the Auxiliary Roman Catholic Bishop of Birmingham, the Right Rev. McCartie, the Commission's president.

The report gives instances of intolerant treatment by the Home Office, particularly over Rastafarian religious rights in prisons. The document also contains a long and...

...sympathetic account of the origins of the Rastafarian movement in Jamaica.

Many of the symbols and the mythology of the movement can be accounted for as a positive response to the West Indian community's historical experience of enslavement, transportation, poverty, immigration to Britain and...

...racial hostility by whites, the report says.

The churches are asked to grant to Rastafarians the same consideration that they show to non-Christian faiths, generally, and the Commission recommends that the Roman Catholic premises should be made available for Rastafarian use.

64 ITEMS "FREED" IN IMPORT LICENCE EASE

SIXTY-FOUR ITEMS, ranging from cutlery to fertiliser, are being removed from the list of restricted imports, "in keeping with the Government's continuing review of import licensing policy".

...

PORTFOLIO SHIFT: WATER GOES TO UTILITIES

RESPONSIBILITY for the National Water Commission and the Underground Water Authority has been transferred from the Ministry of Local Government to the Ministry of Public Utilities and Transport, as from today.

...

PORT - GENTIL
LIBREVILLE

Les deux concerts de Bob Marley à Libreville

Pendant un peu plus de quatre jours, Libreville a été la capitale du «reggae» avec la présence dans ses murs du 2 au 8 janvier 1980 du célèbre chanteur jamaïcain Bob Marley. Ce dernier a cherché à marquer son séjour chez nous par une empreinte : amener les Librevillois à connaître sa musique.

En effet, en plus des entretiens avec la presse locale et autres artistes gabonais, Bob Marley a donné deux grands concerts sous la voûte du gymnase du stade président Omar Bongo. Le premier s'est déroulé vendredi 4 janvier au soir et le second dimanche 5 janvier dans l'après-midi, contrairement au programme qui avait été établi.

Le report du spectacle de la nuit de samedi à l'après-midi de dimanche était dû au simple fait qu'il pleuvait abondamment cette nuit-là et il était pratiquement impossible de faire quoique ce soit. N'empêche que le public venu nombreux plus tôt a été un peu déçu du fait de lui avoir annoncé très tardivement le report du spectacle alors qu'il l'attendait depuis des heures. Qu'à cela ne tienne. Les deux représentations ont été dignes d'intérêt tant il y avait un mélange de rythme, de talent et de grâce.

Le rythme, c'est le reggae» qui, en plus d'un genre musical, est une philosophie, une religion : le talent c'est Bob Marley et son ensemble les Wailers que les Librevillois ne connaissaient qu'à travers le microsillon ou les journaux et qu'ils ont eu le privilège d'être les premiers en Afrique noire à voir en personne; la grâce enfin c'est Betty Wright, un grand nom de la chanson américaine dont l'expression corporelle est de mise sur scène. C'est à elle que revenait chaque fois l'honneur d'échauffer en premier lieu l'assistance. Elle est spécialiste du «Disco»: genre tout à fait différent du «reggae» certes, mais qui retrempait le public composé en majeure partie de jeunes, dans une véritable ambiance de bonne humeur avec des morceaux bien connus comme «Tonight the night», «Ring my bell»...

Quelques minutes de pause et on aura comoris par le dépouillement de cette toile qui surplombe la scène et qui laisse entrevoir un grand portrait de Ras Tafari.

Haïlé Sélassié, roi des rois que les Jamaïcains considèrent comme un dieu, que Bob Marley et ses Wailers sont là. Les cris fusent de toute part et promptement c'est Bob Marley surgit du fond des coulisses, salue, le point en l'air (le salut du pouvoir noir) et c'est le début de «Them Belly full» puis «Rebel music»...

Magistralement soutenu par deux charmantes choristes, Bob Marley chantera, dansera, se propulsera pendant une heure à un rythme débordant de vitalité avec ses nattes virevoltantes qui sont, sur scène, d'un effet très spectaculaire.

Que dire du public sinon qu'il n'a pas réagi comme il le fallait. N'eurent été les interventions répétées du

BOB Marley, un virtuose de la guitare.   (Photo E. Nzame)

Le butane, un gaz rare
Il devient introuvable à Libreville

"... life affirming Rastafari beliefs."
(Rolling Stone/Timothy White)

"Bob Marley was a reminder that there are other realities, other truths ..."
(Charles T. Moses, Newsday, May 18, 1981)

POT LUCK

"Bob Marley was a prophet, a religious and social revolutionary, a messiah who used his burning music not to make millions but to inspire millions with messages of love and liberation. He sang for the 'downpressed' peoples of the world and was idolized by them in return."

(Bill Carlton, Daily News, May 14, 1981)

MARLEY

"He leaves behind a legacy of riddim, goo will, and ju plain love that can never die. The world needed Bob Marley mor than he needed it."
(Rob Santelli, Aquar National, M 19

Los Angeles Times
Opinion
Interpretation   Background
Editorials
PART IV   SUNDAY, AUGUST 14, 1977

Jamaica's Cassandra Sings of Doom and Desolation
Pop Star Bob Marley Serves Up a Mixture of Reggae, Rastafarianism and Revolution

Marley made a wise move in combining his street smarts with his developing business acumen into the establishment of a technically well outfitted 24-track multi-purpose studio at 56 Hope Road, where Bob and various other dreads had lived for the last few years. Tuff Gong International Headquarters, formed in 1979, was just a little distance uptown from the earlier Wailing Souls record shop near Parade and Beeston Streets uptown in the heart of middle-class residential St. Andrew. And a lot of the residents were not too pleased.

With business interests expanding, Tuff Gong opened a newly refurbished record shop and distributions location, in downtown Kingston on the rhythm-packed Orange Street, where the music wares of the likes of Augustus Pablo, Bunny Wailer, Dennis Brown, Gregory Isaacs and Prince Buster are sold.

Both the "Survival" and "Uprising" albums were recorded at Tuff Gong as well as the works of many other established and up-and-coming performers.

Listening to the first playbacks of his recorded sessions at Tuff Gong must have been a celebratory occasion marking an element of independence that Marley had long wanted to savour. He once said to Carl Gayle of "Black Music & Jazz Review", "You've to string de needle if you want to sew somet'ing. . . ." Other pictures show the studio controls, reception area and exterior areas of Tuff Gong at 56 Hope Road.

Because of his influence, the word "reggae", along with the word "Rastafarian", were included in recent editions of the Oxford dictionary. The Rastaman's vibrations were being felt, and acknowledged, even in the academic sphere, the bastion of Western values. They were being felt everywhere.

*   *   *

From where lighting director Neville Garrick viewed things at the technical controls, he could catch all the beats. When interviewed, he gave an inkling of what it must have been like to illuminate a star.

MLW: In Zimbabwe Bob Marley and the Wailers were the main attraction. There were times when you were "support". What was that experience like?

NG: Fleetwood Mac would not like to see us again. We appeared in two festivals with them in Germany where it was billed as Fleetwood Mac and guest. Probably when the show was first announced the posters went so but the radio would cover [the fact that the Wailers were appearing] and the people knew. We perform with them twice and in both shows after Bob's performance, half the crowd walk out. Well we sold in Copenhagen where we played at this place called Tivoli Gardens . . . it is a place where they have ferris wheel and it's like the biggest place for a concert and every year we went to Copenhagen we broke the record. Like we set a record this year, we broke it next year again and eventually broke Abba's highest attendance record. We broke Bob Dylan's record there too.

MLW: People usually have a standard comment on the illusive Black American market to explain why it has not picked up; can you add something?

NG: I think it is something personal going on with that. Because we have made so many attempts towards that market, and at our own expense.

MLW: Like how?

NG: Okay, we played the Apollo Theatre for four nights, seven shows. The amount of money we get for that, we perform at Madison Square Garden one show, same amount of money that you earn doing seven shows at the Apollo, what you call that? We went to the Apollo because we wanted to play in the black community so black people would come, and still 30 percent of the audience was white who found their way uptown at midnight.

We went to Chicago and went and tour *Ebony* Magazine, the Johnson Building, and spend the whole day with them and did an interview, did a photo session, meet the staff in the entire building, you hear me, and *Ebony* has never printed a word about Rasta or reggae music. There was a picture sent once of Dick Gregory kissing Bob's hand when he met him when we did this Amandala show in Boston in May '79 to support freedom in South Africa, and it was the first time [Gregory] met Bob and he was overwhelmed and kissed his hand. [The photo] was sent to *Ebony*, them say it was too humiliating, and I don't understand what they mean by that. Black disc jockeys say it's jungle music. And I don't know if it's not jungle [all of us] come from. Right? And it

Above: Neville Garrick with Bob in Zimbabwe, 1980. Right: Bob rapping with author Malika Lee Whitney (second from left), and Louise Edimo and Manu Dibango in the Cameroon.

can't fit their format. Is only since leading programmers like Frankie Crocker [are] now playing reggae that the others are jumping on it because Frankie Crocker set the trend and when Stevie Wonder sing about it, you have to listen to it. So that is the way that the music is seeping into the black audience. I don't know if it's white people trying to prevent it from getting there or [if it's because] our music is listed new wave music although it's an old story. The way I work it out for myself is that black people is so pressured for day-to-day survival that things that are in the air like message music, go by and pass because is like an ostrich having him head in the ground and him scrounging so much for food . . . whereas a white person have leisure time to relax and hear something and say, hmmmm, them guys different. Them come and check it out. Because although the message is meant primarily for black people it's for everyone who know about oppression. You see it ain't no boogie down or the regular thing where you funky down 'pon weekend 'cos some people say them find it hard to dance to Bob Marley music because them find themselves listening, them feel if them dance to it, it come like them commit a sin, you understand, because you dance to such important lyrics, you know what I mean. Look at "Roots, Rock, Reggae". You listening? Bubbling on the top 100, that mean you don't break the top 100 and you still saying play I on the R&B, want all my people to see, there's a part on the song that never go on the record because it fade out where him say I feel like preaching in the streets of Harlem, want all my people to see. Right? "Now Could You Be Loved And Be Love", "Turn Your Lights Down Low", all on the *Kaya* album, him was begging you to listen. So when Bob do them love songs all him trying to do is get you to listen. If is love song you like, alright, I will drop one on it. Once you listen to that love song, I might get you to listen to the message. Is like you fishing and the fish kinda pick up the little sweet bait and you give him a little length, like, and you just jerk him in.

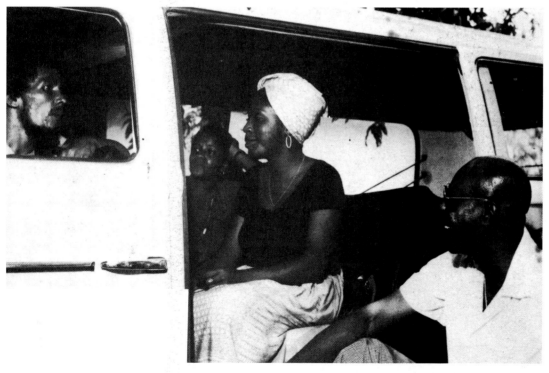

So is the same kinda way, you know. So [Bob] make it blend so it nice, cool and sing 'bout girl and thing. And then them buy the album [because of] one and two tune, and you [can't] only play the two and listen to the rest and so the rest will grow on you.

MLW: Do you think that Bob ever despaired over how long it's taken to get to that audience?

NG: Yeah, yeah, him was worried about that. Him always was quarrelling with the people like at Island Records who deal with the promotion why we can't penetrate through to the black market. You see because first we are marketed to an FM white-oriented thing and that is how reggae broke first. So it wasn't really until Bob put down him foot directly and we had to do it kinda almost ourselves.

161

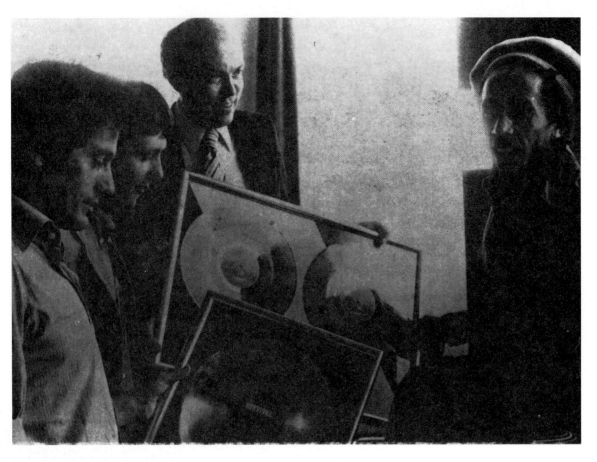

Recognition
that truly
befits a King . . .

Left: Executives of Phor
gram (France—(l-r): Je
Paul Cummin, Jean
Pierre Weiller, Marc
Grande-Mange—make
presentation to Bob for
another milestone achiev
ment in record sales.

Below: Bob with the
Deutsche Schallplatten
award for special achiev
ment in Arnola's black
music division. The awa
is Germany's equivalent
the U.S. Grammy awarc
At the presentation are (
r) Don Taylor, former
manager of Bob Marley
and the Wailers, Monti
Luffner and Alan "Skill
Cole.

Opposite page—top:
Bob being greeted by tof
black American disc joch
Frankie Crocker. Behind
them are Allan "Skill"
Cole (left) and Island
Records' Lister Hewan-
Lowe.

Right-below: Bob auto-
graphing Survival (Af-
rica Unite) albums for
fans—young and old
alike.

Far right: Backstage at
New York's Madison
Square Garden after
another successful engag
ment, Bob is flanked by
Junior Marvin, Mick
Jagger and African pro
moter Mamadou.

> *"Play I on the*
> *R & B*
> *Want all my people*
> *to see*
> *We're bubbling on*
> *the top 100*
> *Just like a mighty*
> *dread"*
> (Roots Rock Reggae)

163

"He that dwelleth in the secret place of The Most High shall abode under shadow of the Almighty."

(Psalm

An ardent lover of sports—especially soccer—
Bob goes through a routine Kung Fu workout
with a friend. Below: in attendance at a
Christmas party for children in London,
1980.

Opposite page: Back from one of his many
overseas trips, a weary Bob converses with
French actress Natalie Delon, and friend and
reggae colleague Jacob Miller. Below: Bob
reads from the Book.

*   *   *

In Jamaica, the vibrations of Bob Marley were felt just as strongly as abroad. They were felt by the poor, whose cause Bob had always championed. His support was not only in words; no, Marley was a man whose bite was just as good, if not better than, his bark. "Skill" Cole would later recall that in just one month Marley gave away $200,000 to various needy Jamaicans at home and abroad. He was always giving—to the Ethiopian Orthodox Church, to hospitals, to schools. . . . As a Trenchtown dweller reminisced, "All you had to do was prove that you really needed the money." While middle class Jamaicans debated over the finer points of Bob's lifestyle—was a BMW consistent with Rasta philosophies, just how many women *did* he have; while they struggled with the idea of his presence in their residential turf (Hope Road)—okay, it's nice to have a superstar as your next door neighbour, but did he *have* to have those other undesirable dreads around him all the time?; while they got enmeshed in their little "isms and skisms", down the road in Western Kingston the poor had no time for that. They knew where he was coming from. They knew where he was going.

So feel this drumbeat . . .
Feel your heart playing a rhythm
And you know it's resisting against ism and skism
Singing I know Jah would never let us down

("One Drop")

Marley's message-filled music, a beginning and an end in itself, a cultural entity, infiltrated other avenues of the island's culture. A Rastaman's vibrations—positive. Most art, by whatever design, reflects signs of the times. Bob Marley was the motivational force to numbers that sophisticated computers could never count.

The National Dance Theatre (NDTC) of Jamaica under the Artistic Direction of Professor Rex Nettleford has nearly done with movements what Bob Marley does with words. The NDTC speaks a body language that is capable of presenting an experience reflecting a near totality of cultural expression, drawn from both Jamaica's immediate and external resources. Professor Nettleford had these words to offer in tribute to Marley:

Above and opposite page: Scenes from 'Court of Jah' performed by members of the National Dance Theatre Company of Jamaica in tribute to Marley.

Bob Marley was of his own kind. Yet he was the direct result and stellar beneficiary of a long and hallowed tradition of that impulsive expression of the creative genius of the Jamaican popular imagination which has always manifested itself in the Jamaican's long-standing quest for self and dignity. He was the beneficiary, above all, of the dread richness of the Rastafarian collective consciousness and like so many other popular artists he appropriated the gift to feed his own remarkable talents as composer, performer and visionary. He, in turn, was to inspire the dance-work *COURT OF JAH* [choreographed by Rex Nettleford for the NDTC] with decor and costume designs by the painter Colin Garland. The dance-work sought to capture the soaring confidence of the majority Black poor, so evident in the mid-seventies, and utilized the now defiant, now celebratory and always deeply reflective music of Bob Marley who was then about to break on to the international scene. The music provided the sounds for the setting of "Court", watched over by a monumental lion, and in which all the children of Jah [the dancers] appear as creatures in a universe where human dignity, nobility of spirit and cultural certitude are the natural possessions of an otherwise denigrated people. Bob Marley asserted that claim in his music and promised redemption to all who had faith.

Another tribute was paid by Mutabaruka, a Jamaican poet, who stamped his own patois meter to a piece, "Wailin," written in 1974, which verbally illustrated the magnitude of the words, sound and power of Marley's musical message vibration.

The influence of Rasta culture on the arts is reflected in the inspiration of works like the N.D.T.C's tribute to Marley, as well as paintings such as the disturbing piece by noted Jamaican artist Osmond Watson (above) and the poetry (opposite) of Mutabaruka (below).

WAILIN

juke box play
. . . an' "stir it up"
in de ghetto
yout'man
      "run fe cova"
hot
hot
      hotter
"curfew" in a trench town
gun a blaze:
      crack
"trench town rock"
juke box playin
. . . an' wi sayin
"long time wi nuh 'ave nuh nice time"
yout'man
      watch yu step
      mek-kase stop
      "screwface"
"lively up yuself"
an' "come reason now"
yout'man
      watch yu ways
"simma down"
      stop frown
play music
play in a "mellow mood"
      music is food
in de ghetto
yout'man
      spread out
      stop bungle
inna "concrete jungle"
      watch it
in de ghetto
hot
. . . hippies smokin pot?
wha dat?
yout'man
      throw wey de
molotov bomb
oppressa-man
      man vex
who yu gwine shoot nex?
hey you big tree
      "small axe"
ready

—MUTABARUKA

"Joseph is a fruitful bough, even a fruitful bough by a well; whose branches run over the wall:
The archers have sorely grieved him, and shot at him, and hated him:
But his bow abode in strength, and the arms of his hands were made strong by the hands of the mighty God of Jacob; (from thence is the shepherd, the stone of Israel:)"

(Genesis 49; 22-24)

CHAPTER II

THE TRIBE OF JOSEPH

They say the blood runs
And it runs through our lineage
And our hearts, heart of hearts divine

("Top Ranking")

RITA...

CONTRARY to many reports that suggested that Bob and Rita Marley were not married before the seventies, including allegations of denials by Bob himself in early interviews, they went to the altar in 1966. Rita Marley is a strong-willed, culturally aware and principled woman who holds fast to the Rastafari faith. She has had to play many roles in the career of Robert Nesta Marley. Being the mother of five, Sharon, Cedella, David ("Ziggy"),

Stephen and Stephanie, is only part of the book she must "fulfill". The children have carved their own niche in entertainment, performing as "The Melody Makers" with four single releases to their credit, "Children Playing In The Street", "Trodding", "Sugar Pie" and "The Plot".

The other chapters of Rita Marley's book are her own pursuits as a solo recording artiste as well as her continuing activities in performing as a member of the I Threes. She has had several single releases, the most successful being "One Draw". *Who Feels It Knows It* is the title of her first album.

As Managing Director of Tuff Gong Records, the chair she now occupies has in front of it a desk piled high with decisions to be made, between answering an incessantly ringing telephone. Somehow, Rita still manages to smile in key.

MLW: How do you cope now that Bob is no longer with us, where do you go for strength?

RM: Well, the main thing is, you know that you are here for a purpose and you have an aim in life and there's a goal after that so you look forward to that. You look forward to a lot of setbacks and struggles both physical and spiritual, because we see all those things in high and low places, and you are alert. Coming from a humble state . . . where you coming from is so important because I think that's a foundation, it is the beginning of yourself, how you come into existence, and when you look through that, you find that you are coming from a poor stage, so you are automatically compelled to be humble and from that you get humility, and that is a guidelight that Bob has used, because if he was of exaltation then maybe he wouldn't be so

effective, as being so humble and going along unobserved. Some people wasn't even listening until now. The flesh that he was wearing he has let off because maybe he has many more reasons than we could be thinking, so that some humility that he has used just rubbed off onto us.

MLW: You are fortunate to have such a loving family. Has this made it easier for you to come to grips with the realities? How have you found the spirit within yourself to explain to them the significance of what has happened?

RM: I tell you, it's the opposite way. It's the children who mainly are the ones explaining to me how to deal with this matter. It's really with their force that I am compelled to. So they are the ones who really give me the positive thoughts.

MLW: Since the foundation has been laid, I think the public would like to know

whether the business ties and musicians' ties will be able to stand up for the Wailers and I Three's?

RM: This is really much too soon to say because I myself will be dealing with other things, trying to keep the Company firm, setting up and re-organizing and there's not much time to look into it. I just ask them to be available for as long as they can. It's not even within our interest, it's in the people's interest. It's the voice of the people that is calling.

MLW: You once told me about the words Bob spoke before he went to rest. Could you reiterate for me?

RM: As I said before, in his songs, in his lyrics, he was telling a reality and he said, "One bright morning when my work is over I will fly away home." And he did that. It was in the morning; the sun was bright. He didn't die because I saw it happen. It was a rest, and I can say that this man is coming again be-

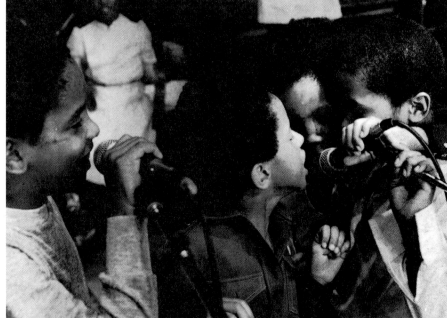

Opposite page: Rita Marley as blushing bride in 1966. This page—top (clockwise): children David (Ziggy), Sharon, Stephanie, Cedella, Jahnesta, Julian, Karen and Kimani pose for a family photo in May 1983. Bob's "tribe" clearly demonstrates their musical talent: centre (l-r)—Rohan, Julian, Stephen and Robert "lively up themselves"; left and above—the much acclaimed 'Melody Makers,' comprising Sharon, Cedella, Ziggy and Stephen, in concert.

173

Bob sharing a light moment with his four children (left). Opposite: Marcia Griffiths, who with Rita and Judy Mowatt, formed the I-Threes.

cause I have been with him, working on the road, and I have never seen anyone work so hard and that's just the physical part of it. In terms of the mental, it is beyond speaking. He delivers himself to the people. He is a people's person. Him get up in the morning, it's people. There is no night for him, no rest. There was always people around, just to be with Bob, talking good or bad, sense or foolishness. There is always people around. So him was really tired, and he was involved in a lot of things which take a mind to deal with. People tried to do a lot of things with him.

He's been on a lot of testing, so I know that for him it's just a phase out in this decade, but he definitely will be coming again because I spoke to him. The morning when I saw that trip I started to sing "Jah will take care of you, he will take care of you, he will take care of you," and him say, "Sing again Rita," and I was shaking him because I saw the trip and I was blowing on him, giving him breath and I was crying . . . but he was there. It was not like say . . . "I am fading." He know what was happening but he was hanging on. The life and the spirit was there and I said, "Bob, don't leave me, don't leave me go nowhere," 'cos I was

on the road, trodding, and him say "Rita, I'm not going anywhere, I not leaving you go nowhere, I'll be with you always," and I talk to him and I sing, and I went to get some juice for I leave him now, he was resting. I laid him down and by the time I reach around the house his mother called and said, "Come, him never wake up," and he went to sleep. But that whole morning, it was a freedom because pain and agony was there. He went through a lot of pain. But no care how them torment and frustrate him with that pain, over that period of time that Bob went through he knew to himself that "this is what I'm going through, this is what is happening to me, I'm hurrying and I'm going with confidence." He had time to assess himself and clear himself, that communication is supposed to be total. You are there and you are here and you have the control.

MLW: I was saying to someone about the gift that we have from the Creator of being able to know what is happening. That feeling that you have. The life tablet that you can see; that's why you could be given those assurances. Because Bob could realize, "I know this is inevitable, this particular part, and it's not the end."

RM: That's what I am here for. I feel fresh and brand new and ready to deal with the continuation of Bob's work, and he even passed it on to his children. Bob has done this [for us]; he died for us, that our sins may be forgiven. When it reach to that point him don't have no part nor lot with you. So long as he can save that soul, not even this [indicates the flesh], but the soul. The flesh is something that the spirit can get out of and leave and if the spirit going [to] leave it, it fall down, it has no value on its own. The spirit plays the most important part. As the song says, you cannot judge a book by its cover. You have to get within. The depths of everything is within. Bob tell his son Ziggy the same day, "The place where I am is beautiful, it's green and fresh, but when I look down on earth there's darkness and doom, but just hold on, unite with people and with mother."

Bob has gone to paradise, he said it, "One bright morning when my work is over I will fly away home." He got that assurance. That is what I experienced, this is my trip with Bob, from that day we still have communication. He promised me that he wouldn't leave me, so he's always here, wherever I am he is always, or "Where thou art, I am also."

MLW: Did he ever say, "Why me?"
RM: Yes, yes. Him say "Wha' de blood-claat,* a wha dis?" But him know. I said, "Bob, it should be me," and him say, "Don't bother say that 'cause what going happen the children?" When we go up on stage me see Bob up there, me say me know You jealous Father, so Your time is anytime, You ready for Your time, so is not like we're on our own here, we are here through the powers of the Most High so we have to give Him His share. That's why when I see so much Rasta bredren and sistren and think of the service of Bob, I gain more confidence because these things we never normally accept but this one was totally different, this feeling of death wasn't there, to say it was a death or a funeral, that feeling was left behind [even with] the black hearse and all of that.

Prophesy say when one man dies, the Lord rejoice but when one is born, mourn because we don't know which spirit going into that flesh, into the mother's womb, so that is the time you most mourn and lament and hope that this one be a good one. But when one pass away, you give thanks to Jah because you know that Paradise is awaiting. I can imagine Bob feel free. I ask Father "Why me," because everything is now left for me, the physical and the material part, so that is my question now, so far the Father is helping to make it much easier. Him left it that way because it's only me could deal with it. Like we say, T-I-M-E. Now we'll see because the shepherd is not directly here. Father say, "All of what you going through now is a test, so be careful. When I am gone be firm, because the fight just begin, the struggle, the work and everything just begin." We're in another era, a new dimension

*Bloodclaat: a Jamaican expletive

now. We can't afford to get too comfortable.

MLW: You are still a young woman with natural needs and wants, do you feel restricted in your role as, for lack of better words, widow?

RM: No, I'm not a widow. I am the type of widow that the system builds on a woman. I am the type of woman who finds myself in a higher and more spiritual and physical realm. That is the privilege that I have found. I haven't lost anything nor anyone.

MLW: Should the time come when you feel the need to make a specific choice, will your decision rest with your personal happiness, that of your family, or how much concern would you have for public reaction with regard to a link that you might decide to make?

RM: How you mean?

MLW: Associating yourself in a marital way.

RM: Personally, I wouldn't confine myself to a marriage, to say that I would get married again and all of that and have that type of life, I just live *[laughter]*, I'm not even thinking about that■

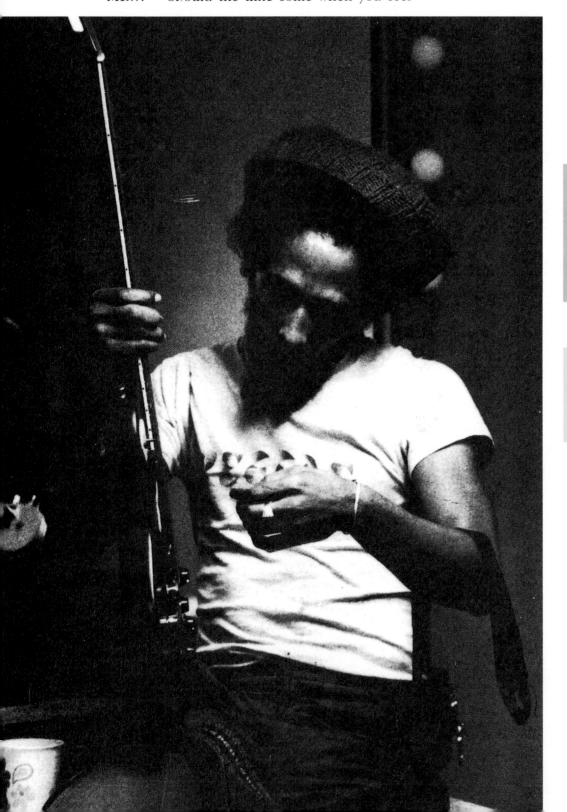

> *"The place where I am is beautiful . . . but when I look down on earth there's darkness and doom . . ."*

"Are you picking up now?"

Mother "B"

Bob's mother, Mrs. Cedella Booker (left) paying tribute to her son in song at the National Arena with assistance from Bob's sister, Pearl (centre) and a friend, Ora.

MRS. CEDELLA BOOKER, or Mother B as she is affectionately called by family and friends, persónifies the typical matriarchal role of a woman in control of things. Mother B has tremendous vision. She will readily share stories about life from a most interesting perspective, and you easily become part of it. Life increased in meaning each time she heard her son Bob's musical report card and she glowed with a love that only a mother could have when he brought home his "O" (outstanding) levels of accomplishment.

MLW: When did you come to grasp that Bob had "made it" musically?

CB: Maybe I don't understand what you mean, but then you see from the time that he write me [in Delaware] he told me he was going to make it.

MLW: In other words, it was long before the public's recognition.

CB: Yeah man, I just see it. Him give me the assurance that one day, you won't have nothing to worry about. I have to say, I feel great. I feel proud when I sit and watch the television and look at all those people and see Bob there with the I Threes and like a voice inside of me say, you made all this possible and I just say, Lord. It carry me away, you know, it make me feel a little way because [of] knowing what I'm looking at, all those people rejoicing, and it just give me more strength.

MLW: You have come in contact with a lot of people who have felt Bob's presence in many ways. What is it you would hope that they would really receive?

CB: There are quite a few people that have written to me personally and it is fantastic. I mean the testimony that they give about Bob and the way that they feel about Bob and the inspiration that they get. To know still that somebody out there can write me or give me appreciation and tell me thanks for the wonderful son, the prophet that I have given to them. I mean it is beautiful. I just love the very action that people give, the way they talk. They have said [Bob's inspiration] has helped them so much, it change their life completely. You know, I get letters from some of his fans and they say the songs give them a new lease on life, and it's so good to know that all this is happening and you can imagine, I feel good.

MLW: What about Bob's relationship with his sister, Pearl, and younger brothers, Richard and Marcus?

CB: Yeah, man, them have a good relationship, you know, because he's like a father to them and he sit down and talk to them. That is why when Bob is away or touring or anything, when him come through, [Miami] is the first place him come to. Before him start the show him come see me and the children because he love them. He was so proud of his little brothers.

MLW: Was there ever a moment when you asked why . . . when Bob took ill?

CB: Yes. I talk to Jah and I would ask Him and I always say to Bob never question because whatever Jah do . . . remember that Jah is mighty and powerful and He could heal you completely with just one look but He don't do that. But one thing I know, that He renew your strength everyday because if He didn't renew your strength you wouldn't be able to outlive this pain, you wouldn't be sick until now, and I sit and pray and pray and I pray and I say who is there to take care of me and the answer was Selassie I. Jah just give me the confidence and I have the same feeling until now. I had the feeling that he wasn't going to [die] . . . and he did. Bob call me one night and him say to me a cancer him have in him toe, and he was very depressed, and I say what and him say yes them say so, and him say momma how me could get all a sickness like that. Jah love me and Jah take care of me, I mean I never do no one no evil, I only do good, so why Jah make me have cancer. The only answer me did have to give him was to say that who Jah love, He chastiseth, because I couldn't find no answer for him, and then me start to pray. And him say, they say [they're going to] cut off the toe and if the cancer is there where them cut it you must hear [immediately they will start to] spread rumour. But you know people say the doctor say is cancer Bob have but me no believe Bob have no cancer and if Bob did have cancer them put it into him, them inject it in him.

Bob never have no cancer. Because me see sometimes when people have cancer. Bob have to go through what him go through because the whole of them who 'round him think him is an ordinary young man or "bwoy"* as them call him, 'cause some of his colleagues when them eat and drink everything that him have, them criticize him and call him "bwoy", you understand me, a little "bwoy", all them things me hear, and pop them big laugh and take no exercise and draw the herb and yet still Bob tolerate them with all this. All that strength to give them food and money and clothing, and when them done, the same ones was criticizing him and underrating him, you understand, so how could he survive with these people that was his worst enemies that was supposed to be his best friends. He couldn't, but he know that these are things that him have to go through.

Him sing "Redemption Song" because he knew the time come for him to depart. Yeah but he was very, very close to his Father and many days [during illness] we read the Bible together and me pray and me pray and me pray and him love to hear me pray and him even tell me to make a prayer record. And me only say yes to him that night and then the next day me say to him what you did say last

night about prayer record, then how that would go, him say you just have to pray all the while and then you play music in between. We just reason together and he was so close to me now, because me could sit and him have him foot in me lap and me rub them and me couldn't get to do that first time from him come outta me sight and is a long time him on him own, but then when me see him come back again me say to him, Bob, you see what the Bible say, once a man, twice a child. Bob was like his picture when he was

eighteen, that was how his locks had come off and they was so pretty, you don't need no brush, you just take your hand.

Bob was just a great young man and I am just so happy that so much people did love him. Me mean the people what really love him, me no talk 'bout the ones that was round Bob, I mean the people where me feel them vibe and me know them love him and it just make me feel good. So many people depend on Bob in Jamaica and when them see them no have nobody to run to again for them wants and when them hungry and whatever, it grieve them heart, you understand, but whatever is to be, Jah will work it out. So all we have to do is wait patiently upon His Imperial Majesty and we just have to see if we can get it together as black people. You see, because Bob paid

*"bwoy": boy, often used derogatively.

him price, Bob suffer the cause to redeem we as Rasta. Bob say how good and how pleasant it is if we would see all the Africans in unity and then we would be strong because him say until we come together we have to suffer. We need to come together, because that's the only way we will be able to make it.

MLW: Were there any special words when Bob must have come to grips with his eventual journey?

CB: That was a great moment. Him call the morning and him ask where is his mother, "Where me madda," and Rita tell

him where I am and Rita call me about 6 a.m. but me decide to get up soon anyhow and Rita say me must come now, now, because she see how him did toss from the night. When me reach and me talk to him, me tell him to move him hand but it not so easy and him [suffering] and you could see him kinda just torment. Him was kinda talking and I was saying to him why you talking so loud and me say I know you happy you in Miami now. So me was there fixing the thing in his nose,* that was the Saturday, so every time me put it, it lean and him say, after every time you take your big hand it no must drop out, and him joke and him talk to Rita and them, that time him done bless the pickney** them and him take them on the bed with him and him bless them. Him must tell Cedella [his daughter] to fan him because him

*respirator
**pickney: children

hot all the while even when the air conditioning on, that was the Saturday.

But then the Monday morning, I went there. When I went I saw some nurses inside there and the nurse finish and him say momma and me say, yes, son I'm right here, and me go up to him and me say, how you feel this morning and him say pain, pain. Me say me bring some things for you to drink and him say him no want it yet. So afterwards him say come here and me did stand up beside and him say come close and me go right up to him to the bed and him take me hand and him hold me hand and [the left] hand couldn't move and him squeeze me and when him squeeze me, me no squeeze him back, but when him squeeze me, him can't squeeze me hard but he try him best, because we used to do this, you know. Make him squeeze me hand to make sure how good him can use his hand and sometime him squeeze me to about that [indicating strength which is very slight] and then after that him do like this, him shake, but me never want him to feel is a shake hand him give me and me start brush and rub him hand and then him let me go. And then him say him want some water and me give him some water and him drink it and about five or seven minutes pass and me give him some carrot juice and him drink it off.

That time the people say them [going to] take some x-ray and then them carry the x-ray come and him say stay close to me and [the nurses] try to prop him up and me go round to the other side and him say don't make them make me drop off, and we say we not going let them do that. And then after them finish them say them [going to] give him a needle and [Bob] say yes because him want to sleep and then when him lie down, is just like him just pull the [respirator] out of his nose. He didn't need this anymore. After him pull it out him make it go sideways and I say put it back, it will help you to breathe while you taking your rest. So when me try it out, me couldn't put it so me go call the nurse and him just go off and poor Rita wasn't there. The time Rita come you know and him just sleep . . . .

Me see him get that deep breath because his breath was very short and then from the time him go out so and [makes the sound] ugghhhhh, I say no way for him to come back, him gone too far. The

breath gone too far. It must cut off some-where down the line because it was very deep and long because that time he was travelling then and I was saying some prayers for him and I was singing, I know the Lord will make a way, and he will take care of you. And then I pray and tears start run down while I was praying and him say don't cry for me, you hear, don't cry for me, I'm alright. And me say to him, son, me not crying for you, and I pray, I was talking to Jah and I ask Jah to release you from the pain and this is how my joy, my tears, flow, and him say awoah.*

And it make you feel so good and so strong and . . . him just fly home to [the Father] . . . and then when him pass and I look on him and Diane [Jobson, lawyer and personal assistant] say Miss B? he not breathing, I was just as calm as cucumber and she say he's not breathing and then me say let me call the nurse and I say please come check Mr. Marley, and she came and she looked at him and she said, I think he's deceased, and Diane said what, no, no and she said call the doctor and he came and they said he's deceased, take him and put him to another floor, and then while he was there for a little while, that time the nurse take up the things and Rita came and my God, it was a terrible time for her; she was there in the morning but just at that time, I think she went to get something for him, and then she start to cry. No tears could come to my eyes. I feel like how I feel here now and he look so handsome; and then I go and I talk to him and ask him to direct me, to give me strength, to give me love, I said you know we have tried, we have tried, we all love you, and the Father love you more now you gone away, but I know even this, this *[indicating skin]* corrupt.

*awoah: "That's alright, then."

Because he couldn't get better, because he couldn't be in that body again.

Bob have to go through this, and today we should rejoice because Bob has paid the price so that Rastafari can be recognized and his message has been preached all over the world, so who accept them accept it already and who reject it nobody can't say well them never hear. But him only glad that the message spread. And now that he's gone people just look into and plenty people who wasn't even conscious of what was the true message start look. Bob is love, so much love can't bring sorrow that kind of a way. Let love shine, when sorrow come, love must lick out sorrow, seen.* Everytime me think me going to start to feel sorry little tears come. Him don't want to see me shed a tear. Something just come and dry up me tears immediately■

*seen: "understood?"

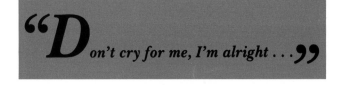

"**D**on't cry for me, I'm alright . . ."

Cindy...

SCANDAL sheets and gutter tabloids were always quick to recount whatever social adventure Bob Marley was rumoured to be involved in. One of the more sensational headlines so far as the public was concerned was the saga of "Beauty and the Dread", Marley's involvement with 1976 Miss World Beauty Contest winner Cindy Breakspeare, who also bore him a son, Damien. (She is now married to Senator and Attorney, Tom Tavares-Finson, and runs a successful craft business, called Ital Craft.)

It is common knowledge that Marley had many children outside of his marriage with Rita. However, he did honour the commitment that bearing fruit carries. One can be sure that when he sang "not one of my seeds shall sit on the street and beg bread," he meant it.

From her treasure of memories, Cindy recounts aspects of the compassionate experience that had a lot more substance to it than most people would care to imagine.

MLW: How did your relationship with Bob begin?
CB: That started a long time ago. In the days when Tuff Gong was not Tuff Gong, when the property was still owned by Chris Blackwell. Fifty-six Hope Road was separated into little individual flats and my brother Stephen and I occupied one and Bob and the Wailers used to rehearse in a room at the back of the premises. And they were there so much and so often that they began living there and

Cindy Breakspeare Tavares-Finson—winner of the Miss World Beauty Contest in 1976—with son, Damien.

that was how I came in contact with Bob initially. In those days I hardly knew Bob at all. I couldn't identify him any different from the other dreads that were in the yard, they were always playing football and such and eventually times and things changed and I became changed and I became a fan of his music. My brother had *Catch A Fire* and then we got *Natty Dread* and Dicky Jobson came in and showed us the album jacket before it came out and I began to be aware of Bob as a musician, as a writer, and apparently as somebody who seemed to be a special person. And since we were living in the same yard, from there, it just grow.

MLW: There is a tendency to question the genuineness of a relationship like that. The caste and class system of Jamaica doesn't always make certain twains meet. One might think that it was an effort on your behalf to relate with someone who was a little more "grounds" than your upbringing allowed.

CB: Well, when doors close everybody is just people, you know. When you get right down to basics, it's not about class or creed. I think in fact, though, there might be times when Bob might be doing something that he felt I would have no interest in and he wouldn't care to take me into those circles and there were times when I might be doing something that wouldn't have interested him either and he would not have felt comfortable in that situation either. There were times when there was no common ground for us to meet on. But there will always be a common ground between Bob and me regardless of what these things are. I think that the point that people usually try to make, they don't understand themselves what it is. It's not so much that you are a lower class or I am a higher class, or I am a lower class and you are a higher class. It is that we have grown up differently. And things that you take for granted, I don't quite understand, and things that I can expect, you know nothing of, and that is where you get that sort of seesaw where I want from you something that is not in your nature to give.

MLW: Did your conscience bother you in terms of Bob's other commitments? I'm referring to Rita and his family.

CB: Well initially, yes, it did bother me. Anyway it was his mother who finally told me that they were in fact married and she spoke as though she thought that I knew about it long ago and then she thought she was letting the cat out of the bag, but by then Damien was already on the way and it was too late at that point in time to really turn around and run in the opposite direction, so you just go through.

MLW: With both of you being outgoing, how did this affect your privacy?

CB: Bob was like that, in that he didn't care to have any woman that he considered his woman around all the time when he had to be dealing with everybody, fans, press, followers, members of the band, whatever. There were times when he would just like to move through on his own, and to be totally receptive to everything that was always going on around him. I think he always feared jealous women and things like that although I was never that type. If things didn't suit me I just go *[indicating movement]* in the other direction.

MLW: You were kind of displayed in a way that Bob, as a Rastaman, would take exception to. How did that affect the relationship, or did it? I mean, his prized possession on public view . . .

CB: Well I suppose he had other prized possessions that weren't on public display; I mean, you know everything is relative. But I think for him it was more difficult than for me because he always used to call me Miss World. And he would always make a point of saying, well how the training going nowadays and the fitness, because he was a lover of fitness, not just from a vanity point of view but from a health point of view.

And I know that to be able to claim Miss World as your lady was something that any man would be proud to do, so Bob was no different in that respect, but I don't think that he especially agreed with the Miss World thing but he wasn't the kind of person to try and stop you. He just tried to encourage me in other areas when they eventually came along, like Ital Craft. He would never try and fight me down if I'm going through with something, but when he sees an area where he can encourage me and he feels that is better and more constructive, now *that's* when you get some support, you get *encouragement,* you get everything, more tools, more shelves and more craftsmanship, you could never want [anything more] because that was something that he really believed in and thought was good.

MLW: It's natural for every woman to want to know and to feel that she is important. What gave you your indications?

CB: A lot of different things, his behaviour towards me. Bob and I had a sort of mutual respect for each other, apart from romanticism or emotional things, we had a mutual respect. I always tried to tell him exactly what I thought, though, and not just with respect to me but with respect to him and to anything, I always tried to deal in a very sort of forthright manner and leave the hero worshipping for the fans. Everything on a one-to-one basis, you have your international ac-

claim and so forth but you are still a man. This is how I see it and maybe you don't like to hear what I have to say, but I say it anyway. And I was often told by people close to him, people inside the group, whenever they would listen to Bob and I discuss something, [that] they always felt that we had a good rapport and that the way I would express myself was a good thing in dealing with Bob because he agreed with that forthrightness.

MLW: What was the basic complication in maintaining a relationship like that?

CB: He spread himself too thin. Too many children. Too many ladies. Too many commitments. Too much work. Too much people. Everybody wanted something from Bob so it meant that everyone that was close to him was sort of a quarter way satisfied. They never saw enough of him and the time when they did they were ready to cuss him because he never got there the day before. He was in a vicious circle, a very vicious circle, and as a woman in his life, one would always feel, well, I wish I could leave out the cussing and just say wha' happen bredda Bob, nice to see ya. There were times when you *did* do that, certainly, but there were times when [it was], what happen to ya, I thought you were coming to lunch yesterday, what happened to you? But maybe ten people from Trench Town were descending on him and begging him money to build a wall outside some organization; God knows that he was busier than the Prime Minister, that's all I can say to that.

MLW: How did the leave-taking occur? Did you, did he or did it just wane itself?

CB: We never decided. It got to a point where Bob was away so much and we were seeing so little of each other that to me it didn't make sense. It just did not make sense. I loved him dearly, not only as Damien's father or somebody that I felt had inspired me greatly, taught me a lot of important things even about being a woman, and [for] a man to teach you about being a woman, that's pretty good. But we couldn't really have a relationship going, a consistent relationship. It just kinda phased itself into a friendship, a respect. When I heard that he was ill, I said regardless of everything, now is the time that he needs some support, and I felt that of all the people that he may know, or may be romantically involved with now, I am someone whom he knows, and as it turned out, Rita and I ended up spending a month together in New York in the flat taking care of him. She answered the door and I cooked and if she had to go out, she would say, well hold the fort until I come and vice versa and that was how it was. Because we both knew him well enough to be around him at that time even though it was a strain for everybody.

MLW: Bob speaks to everyone individually in his music. Is there any particular song that you felt was addressed to you personally?

CB: Well, I know "Turn Your Lights Down Low" he wrote for me personally and he told me and I remember when he wrote it. He sat out there [in the yard] and he played it and I was in my room and I heard it and a long time after we really talked it out, because on the album, *Kaya*, there are many love songs and there were many that were not especially directed to me. They were just a vibe or a feeling that he had at that time, but that one in particular, I know.

MLW: When did you first find out about the cancer diagnosis?

CB: Not until October last year [1980] when it was diagnosed in the lung and the brain. I was not with Bob when they operated on his toe for the cancer there, I was off on a five-week trip. That was in 1977, and by the time I reached on with him in

from me. I couldn't let him use my record player so I gave him one of his own and he's just taken over my whole collection and he plays them, and he has a guitar and he knows [the songs] and he sings them.

MLW: In terms of a lasting reflection, how would you sum up your relationship with Bob?

CB: Boy, that's a once-in-a-lifetime thing. Really! Definitely. Because there were certain things that he taught me that were very definitely imprinted in my mind, in my soul, and nobody would have to teach me that again.

MLW: What sort of thoughts do you have of Bob now that time has nurtured things?

Miami at his mother's home, I asked him what really happened with the toe, he said is cancer them say me have but me don't believe it. That was how he always approached it. It was something that he really didn't want to deal with.

MLW: Did you still maintain a degree of communication with him when the relationship dissolved?

CB: Yeah man.

MLW: I know Damien is quite young [four] but does he know who his father is?

CB: Most definitely and positively. Daddy? Are you kidding? He has all of his records and as a result of taking them away

CB: I think I understand the person that he was a lot better now when I can sit back, look on and assess. When you get together with someone, you really don't know everything, you don't know everything about their childhood, their upbringing and as time goes by . . . . Time went by during our relationship and I learned more about how Bob grew up and so forth; I understood then how and why he handled his personal relationships the way that he did and why it was impossible to sort of form one total attachment to one person. He never grew up that way.

He lived away from his mother for a long time, he lived here, he lived there so it was kind of a situation where he had to live for the here and now and what is happening now, and he [would] just go through with that and that is your experience. That is what has been given to you and you just go through with it. It's not about thinking about when I reach back to that one or when I reach back to the other one, as a youth growing up he never knew when he was going to reach back to anybody, so you just take what is coming now and it manifest itself all

ner or not. Bob was somebody whose inspiration was so great and people's love for him was so great that he was constantly giving to everybody, so he could never just drop everything at 7 o'clock and, say, do what you wanted him to. He just couldn't do it. He might find himself writing a song and you better believe that he is going to show you plain that when the music lick, is just music. All dinner, all girl, all everything else wait, the music come before everything else. Those things, he would never sit me down and say Cindy, you are to appreciate your

through his life. There were so many people offering and wanting all the time that I don't see how he could have really kept himself away from that. I understood him a lot better, the fact that he could never really tell you, well I will be there at 6 o'clock and at 6 o'clock you see him coming through the door, things like that, and eventually I just realized that Bob would probably be someone for me to love from a distance and not try to live with on a close basis.

I wanted a more stable relationship that conformed, family life, well, are you going to pick the kids up from school or am I. Things that you know have to be done and so on, are you coming for din-

inspiration and you are always to respect it . . . never . . . but when you observe the way that he lived and the way he appreciated his inspiration and the way he spoke, he always gave it number one priority above everything else. If you have something inside of you to come out and other people can appreciate it in some creative form or whatever, just go there with it. He was not a preacher in that sense, but if you take an example from the way he lived you learn a lot of things.

MLW: Much of his inspiration came from his embracement of Rastafari; what did you draw from his beliefs?

CB: Well, just a more natural way of life. In

terms of your food, your habits, self-respect as a woman, appreciation of your children, I mean you're going to love them anyway so you think about it a little more, or [those] who may want and don't have [what they need]. I think especially when I was Miss World, because that is a role that can go in a lot of different directions and I always look to him as a sort of rock to give me a certain strength to be going in a good direction [so] that, okay I am going to take advantage of the year, I am going to make as much money as I can but I am not going to degrade myself to do so, I'm not going to accept things that really and truly are not up to a certain level. He was always there. I didn't find myself running around with a lot of nutty nutty people, people who you are not sure is "he, she or it" 'cause you have plenty *[laughter]* of those out there. So [Bob] gave me a very firm foundation there. I kept saying, well, will Bob approve of this?

MLW: Did Bob ever come to you with the suggestion to read a chapter a day from the Bible?

CB: Yes, and we used to read. I began and I reached where all the chronologies are, where you have all the families where he begat and he begat right down the line and I put it down and I never took it up again. But we used to read and when he was ill I used to read to him from the Bible. I used to read to him like from Job. But I think Bob was a person who understood [what happens] if you try to ram something down a person's throat, and you could teach them good ways and good values without necessarily insisting that they read a chapter from the Bible a day.

I had a Roman Catholic upbringing, I went to a Roman Catholic convent from the age of ten years. I went to church so much and I had so much religion all the time, before and after class, first thing in the morning, rosary in the evening, benediction on a Sunday, mass every morning, a *lot,* so to really get me in church, boy, you have a hard time. So he realized that to try to play too heavily on the religious aspect, it would turn me off. I learned a lot from his religious beliefs and I don't tell you I believe everything that Rastafari believe, but it has given me a lot of inspiration, a lot of direction because it reminds me, when things go right I look up and I say give thanks. It kind of put me back in touch with just the fact that there is a Supreme Being, there is a Creator and we are all beholden to

the Creator, and whatever good and so forth you have to really appreciate.

MLW: Now you are the mother of Damien, Mrs. Finson, and the proprietress of Ital Craft, is there any void in your life?

CB: No. I have one or two secret ambitions that I will not disclose at this particular time but the only void I feel, like perhaps where Bob is concerned, is for Damien. Well, Bob has certainly left us a lot to draw on; he left us a lot of things to think about, a lot of words to listen to and to think about what it is he's trying to point out.

But boy, I sure wish he was still around, you know what I mean, I really, really do. I know a lot of people share that feeling. But especially for Damien, he knew him but was never really able to be with him over a period of time and really understand what made Bob tick and what a big person he was, what a natural person he was. It wasn't that kind of situation. [Any Jamaican, even someone like Thomas [Tavares-Finson, Cindy's husband], loves Bob. Because Thomas was like that too, you know, because the area and the constituency that he works in is a ghetto. He deals with all the same people where Bob is coming from so he knows exactly what the pressures are, what the problems are and they are just dealing with it from different areas, you know what I mean.]

MLW: Can you recapture how you felt the first time you heard the music again after Bob's transition?

CB: No, because when I play it now, I still feel same way and that feeling wasn't a one and only feeling, it follows through right until this day. When I buy *Chances Are* and I listen to it, is like I'm just hearing his music for the first time. I wouldn't say that was an isolated thing; and like how Damien just play the music morning, night and noon; I tell you, as fast as batteries run out, he say, mommy more batteries for the record player. So Bob is ever present and that isn't something that I would try to fight or a feeling I would try to push out. It is something I can draw on. It is something that I revel in. He never lived to be an old man but he lived a full life. A man who came from nothing to everything. From total poverty to riches which were love and adoration∎

"If you take an example from the way he lived, you learn a lot of things . . ."

'SKILL'...

ALLAN "SKILL" COLE was a man to whom Bob Marley gave a special hearing. His being one of the more visible and lasting associations, Skill recounts the beginning and the extensions of that association.

MLW: You are a man who has received a certain degree of recognition as a great football player. You were also very close to Bob. When did your association begin?

SC: In the early sixties when Bob just [started to] record. I love listening to good music. And at one time when Bob was going through a period and him have a problem, I started to manage them. This was after I came from North America where I was playing in a football league. Bob had just come back from Delaware and him did dread first and trim and come back.

MLW: Were you ever present when Bob was writing?

SC: Most of the album like *Natty Dread, Rastaman Vibration,* is me and him alone. Even "War", me is the man who come carry the speech of His Imperial Majesty and give Bob and tell him to sing it.

MLW: You were exposed to more of Bob's intimacies and personal convictions. Did you feel part of his musical struggle?

SC: Well, him tell me personally, me is the only one who really help him with his music. Me no like give myself credit but me is the only man who make him get three No. 1 tunes straight. "Trenchtown Rock" was the first, "Dem Belly Full", and "3 o'clock Roadblock". Is me really promote them because in those days the record system was so dirty that you find if you don't go through them, you don't get airplay and so me take up me initiative as manager and me see that them get proper airplay.

MLW: I read somewhere that you roughed up some radio station people . . .

SC: Yeah, you have to do it, because if you don't do it in those days as Rasta . . . we get [nothing but] fight from the big companies. Them always want the artiste to come to them, to exploit the situation. So I tell Bob the best thing is to fight it and him fight it. But is a whole heapa fight with the radio station because certain people don't want to see the tune as Number One because we going to sell. It cause problems but me is a man if me do things, me do it with me heart, so me have to get involved and that cause a whole heapa things. We really come revolutionize music, the industry.

MLW: "Rat Race" was a tune that got banned. You couldn't do anything about that?

SC: No. Government ban them and we as Rasta, we couldn't fight the Government at that time because all of the people [in the record system] was controlling the so-called bureaucrats. Can't really fight them. [They were not too keen on us] but yet now, as you see, times change.

> **"H**im is a clever youth, you know . . .**"**

MLW: You were off the island for extended periods. When you were away, how did you keep up communication?

SC: Well, Bob come check me one time in Africa, so me keep in contact and follow him progress and what was happening.

MLW: Did you feel removed?

SC: When we move from Bob, certain forces come in. Because [I feel that] when I was with Bob, certain things couldn't happen. [If I was with him to make sure he exercised,] he couldn't get sick 'cos his body would be in good condition.

MLW: When you left Africa, did you come to Jamaica first?

SC: I joined [The Wailers] in Europe, that was the 1980 tour.

MLW: You said that perhaps if you were present Bob wouldn't get sick. Who directed him to seek medical care in the West? Why

wasn't he treated elsewhere like Jamaica or Africa?

SC: Bob became very popular since 1977 and [he became] *the Reggae Star.* But [because] Bob grow so big, some of the people around him was more exploiting the situation, and Bob was so popular and making all this money that them never care 'bout his personal welfare, like him health. Because my bredren who used to [visit him] tell me that [Bob] stop eat, him couldn't get no time to eat, the people them 'round him so. So you find [that] his body break down. And that is what happen to Bob, he wasn't eating enough food and not getting enough rest and everybody around him and pushing everything to him, him couldn't hold it. Bob is a musician, you know. Bob is not even a business man to that, yet him is a man who have a business head. Him is a clever youth, you know. Certain things him couldn't take. Him so proud that if him

know something affect him he not going say it, him just keep it inside him.

MLW: The injury to his foot, in an earlier diagnosis it was revealed as cancer . . .

SC: [Let me] tell you what happen. In about 1970 or 1972 Bob [was playing] football and a bredda* step on him toe. When him come off of the field in the evening and him lean 'pon the car, him take off him boot and the toe stay a little way, him had to wear sandals couple days because it did get a little way and it take a little time to get better. Now when I was in Ethiopia now, I get a message that this toe business come up again and the doctor want to amputate the foot or something, and when them did the x-ray them find him have third stage melanoma. Third stage melanoma means that it had metastasized or begun to spread severely. So now what I understand from the doctors is that at that stage the only thing that them could do is remove the nail. Some wanted to amputate the foot but that still wouldn't stop nothing. What them found out to be the best thing was to build him up with antibiotics. I remember when him show me the toe when him come to Africa, me see a tired man in Africa and I tell him him look tired. That was in 1978. When you look in his face you look at a man who was well worked. Them work Bob too much. *Those* people work him too much. Look like everybody 'round him was on a trip, you dig. Nobody was around him to say, hey Skip,* you want a little rest. Him get advice from people outside but him never take it. But now, the people who work with him and go 'round 'pon tour should [have told] him, but everybody was on a trip.

MLW: Did Bob confide in you that the cancer analysis had been made when he came to see you in Africa?

SC: Him tell me 'bout the toe. But if you know how him rest, if Bob feel a pain, him [won't] tell you. Him so proud, but him say them want to take off him toe and him say him can't deal with that.

MLW: When Bob's condition became critical, were you summoned directly or did you just come on your own?

SC: I [saw] Bob in London. The first thing he and me do in London is go jog and cool off. Me see him do a lap and him tired and me say [this is] madness because the last time me and him jog was during a

*bredda: brother
*Skip: familiar term generally used to address someone, equivalent to the American "Joe", for example.

tour in Germany in 1976 and me tell you we run for about an hour and a half and him was in top condition, and [this time] me see him run one lap and him tired, and me say Rasta, me don't like how you stay, how you unfit, and him start tell me a whole heapa things.

MLW: After Bob's collapse in Central Park in September 1980, which you witnessed, who initiated calling Dr. Issels from Germany?

SC: Well after we go to Sloan Kettering in New York, Bob go to Cedars of Lebanon in Miami, because that's where he was the first time with the toe, and them diagnose the same thing and them say the best place is Sloane Kettering. So Bob and me and Dr. Carl "Pee Wee" Fraser go there and them [at Sloane Kettering] just want Bob to stay there and . . . them start give him radiotherapy and it poison him system a little way. So now the American Cancer Society have this big seminar where all these specialists attend. So we manage to get through some of the security and we find out Issels the best man on record so we decide to give him a try and we reason it out and we really reach Issels now after a whole heapa barriers and obstacles. That was November. They start the radiotherapy in October and then the chemotherapy.

MLW: Had Bob's locks come off?

SC: No. When him get the chemotherapy it start look a way and it scratch him. Boy, one morning I leave him and the night me come back and I don't see no hair 'pon him head.

MLW: Did they have to go inside his head?

SC: No, the way that tumour was, the only thing according to them was the radiotherapy because if [the tumour] burst it would be more serious. But his speech . . . what happened was his left side . . . it kinda get a little way. It wasn't easy for him to walk, him couldn't walk, the left foot never move in motion the right way. But I see some great improvement with Issels after the first five, six weeks and him start walk. Him start walk an hour and a half in the Bavarian Alps in Germany, where he was being treated.

MLW: Did he ever speak to you about the treatment?

SC: Only one day him say when him did walk, him say why him never hear of Issels from the first. Me know Issels the best man. Me tell you me see improvement in the first six weeks and Bob just say why him couldn't hear 'bout Issels from the [beginning], him could [be cured] now.

MLW: When did Bob's final regression begin?

SC: What was happening, him did have a tumour, a large tumour over him lung and that is what was giving the problem, because with all the treatment Issels couldn't stop that. The doctor used to control it for a time, but that one was so aggressive that when we look 'pon the x-ray, the small one disappear but the big one, like another month and a half after, two months after, in the x-rays we saw it was like something expanding, you know, like a woman's belly.

MLW: Did Bob ever express surprise to you about the fact that he could get such a disease?

SC: Well what them say [is that] it was a rare type of melanoma, which is rare among black people. Him wonder if it in him foreparents because them say you can

inherit it, so them say. Me personally don't know. Me only know Bob is a man who . . . when you become prominent in this society you mustn't open up yourself to that extent. You have to be careful because you get popular and a man hate you.

MLW: What about Issel's commitment in terms of the special care Bob required?

SC: People at the clinic was complaining because Bob was on special priority and the doctor wanted to win Bob's case. A case like that could get him more recognition but him always say this case was very hard. Issels was doing everything everyday, and Bob did see that because Bob was going to him twice a day, even when the [other] people gone home him used to get treatment, that will show you the type of interest.

MLW: Did Bob ever say, I don't want any more needles or treatment or . . . ?

SC: No, no, him just say from him born him never know him could get so much injections. And we did start show him the Bible. Not every man understand the mystery of death. Most of the man who say them is Rasta don't understand the mystery of death because them don't read the Bible and some of them who do read the Bible from Genesis to Revelation still don't want to accept what them read, knowing that this mortal body must go down. For as Paul say, for a seed to live it have to die. Before him really pass, me show him them things, the mortal body go down but in the resurrection a man rise, so the whole teaching go, and every man no matter who him is, man born must taste of death and that me really try to get through to him as a man who done read the Bible twice and try show him, and him accept it.

MLW: Did Bob ever say to you that he was prepared to leave his flesh?

SC: No, no, him not going say that because you see when me 'round Bob, him feel strong and I stand near him and say to everybody, Roots*, and him reply—firm. We try build him everyday. Me carry him to the clinic everyday . . . and [along with another Rasta brother] we try encourage him that a man must have the will to live regardless of what him go through. Me show him [that this message was in] certain Bible stories.

MLW: So would you say that his faith was ever tested?

SC: No, not when me was there, all me did say was hey Rasta, me just want you to read the Bible. Him suppose to finish him Bible, but enough diversion around him. A Rastaman duty that, that him must try to read his Bible from Genesis to Revelation so that he understand. For His Imperial Majesty say that. How to solve your future and present problems, how to confront them, what to expect. So that's why my emphasis on him was to just read. Me understand the situation that Bob was in. Death is something that must come. Physical death. But now legends never die, you know what I mean. Me show him them things there. Because when a man in them situation, him want confidence. Me try my best and the doc'. Me show him the scroll. Me no talk 'bout

*Roots: Rasta greeting affirming that everything is all right.

no personal thing. Me talk 'bout what God inspire man to write thousands of generations ago, and me know him understand that.

MLW: At what point did the doctor . . . ?

SC: Give up? When I spoke to Issels after the fluid start flow in the lung, and Bob start get weaker and weaker and there was nothing more Issels could do. Him get critical. Bob start come down and that was it.

MLW: Were you in Germany at the time?

SC: No, but I used to call Issels like every two days. I did because I want to know what go on, dig.

MLW: So what was your last communication with Bob?

SC: Me talk to him a couple days before him leave Germany. On the phone. He was very weak.

MLW: In terms of a lasting reflection, what do you have that is alive that you received from Bob?

SC: Is one thing I know . . . him is a man to an extent where, when you hear him say certain things, him try to live to it. Him is a youth with enough integrity. And him is a fighter too.

MLW: It must be a very heavy emotional thing to watch your bredren [depart] . . . feelings that define what man is supposed to be.

SC: Yeah. Me look at it and even one night me even get away and go back to me bed, me just check it out and me say boy, [Bob] just really start to expand the way him really suppose to expand. A young tender age like that him just start mature, him just start make some money and start live so . . . me sorta feel it more than him. Because it bring tears to me eyes [some] nights. Me just look 'pon him. A youth [who was] innocent, you know what I mean . . . and me really see certain

JAH LIVES

things happen to him and me start really wonder, say boy . . . I look into it and me just have to say, the Lord knows best. Me tell you the truth, me really feel it.

MLW: How do you reason with Bob now?

SC: Right now? One time I pick him up since him pass away. At one time me get a little sighting [while I was resting], you know. A vision [that I got] in a night rest. Him alright. We only pray [that] him is in the bosom of Abraham and we pray that him should rest in peace.

MLW: Do you feel a void within yourself?

SC: You see, hear me now. Me see Bob different from most ones because some see Bob and them afraid of him. But me see him as me bredren. As me bredda where most things him tell me, him don't tell a next man. And boy it hard, is like sometimes you can't believe it. Like sometimes when you hear certain music, is like him still there. Yet me know the music live. But it really take a time to really overcome certain things. But [since] we is Orthodox we understand. Bob lives. There's this old saying and me say it already, that legend don't really dead. Legend never die, them live on, and Bob is in that category. Me feel him more time you know. Me feel him. All when me hear certain music me remember when we used to sit down and him play it [one] night-time. All up at Hope Road when everybody gone to bed, me and him alone. All them things will go down as history and him record it.

MLW: What would you sight as Bob's world mission?

SC: Bob was the foremost ambassador who really spread Rastafari. No other man 'bout the place do that so far. Him open up enough people to Rasta. All different nationalities, which is a great job. Him was . . . as I say, him was ambassador, unsurpassed, you know what I mean. Me really glad one of our bredren come do that because somebody had to do it and God chose him to do it and him really tell the people of Rastafari to the best of his ability. And you find people get aware of Rasta, the people who was rejecting and dejecting it in this society. Now you find is a different situation through people like Bob and maybe even me too [because I am] the first dreadlock to play football for Jamaica . . . and Bob now, look what him do international. Him do a great job and the Book say you must show me your works. God say faith without work is death. Him do a good work.

MLW: On a universal scale, what do you see as Bob's main contribution?

SC: Well you see, in Africa, in Zimbabwe. Bob's lyrics, them appeal and them wake up more of the oppressed people of the world, and the majority of the world suppose to be oppressed. Especially for Third World countries. Them more see him as a messenger. His music relate to the trend of things, to events. Some people in Africa tell me when Bob sing is like is them him [is talking] to. Him really reach to people in oppressed countries who get to hear and see as a man who come to sing, to liberate them personal self. Him music go to the mind■

Judy...

You've been so good to me
And I thank you sincerely
In my state of unrighteousness
You came to me and my soul was blessed
Through you I've gotten my first inspiration
For writing my songs into the light of salvation
You are a father, a brother
One that I've never had
And I thank God for you—for you I am so glad
The archers have shot arrows at you
Sorely grieved you
But your bow, abode in strength
When the enemies came your angles were descent
They don't know you are here for a purpose
Like the famine in Egypt your corn is still feeding us
Oh father, brother, one we've lost
Now we've had
We thank God for you
For you we are so glad
Joseph we love you
Joseph we love you
Joseph we love you

("Joseph")

Dedicated in love by Sister Judy Mowatt from her album *Black Woman* © Ashandan music.

JUDY MOWATT, member of the I Threes, and a song goddess of magnificent spiritual beauty, reflects her true experience of being in the presence of Bob Marley, which signalled a change from her earlier style of recording.

MLW: How did you make the transition from the soul kind of sound to the more message-oriented music when you began singing with Bob Marley and the Wailers?

JM: I used to sing a lot of soul music, sometimes rhythm and blues. Bob has done a lot for me because in listening to his lyrics I have learned to view life not from just one perspective. I've noticed Bob's science, and how Bob deals with music, and from then I began to write.

MLW: Was there any particular music that influenced you?

JM: No, I would say all of them, because every one you listen to is not dealing about just love. It deals with a situation with a Rude Boy, it deals with a situation of a youth being shot down in the street, a woman lamenting and needing to be reassured like "No Woman No Cry". A lot of people used to tell me when I travel that they can communicate with Jamaica through Bob's music. So when I look at how he really formulates his lyrics, I know that there was something more than just singing about I love you man. There was something more than just singing songs that do not relate to you at all. Because most people are singing songs just to make money but not to uplift the people's moral standards. If Bob was just an ordinary singer, people wouldn't accept him, but it's the philosophy that he had.

MLW: Did you share those early creative moments with Bob when you were writing?

JM: When I wrote "Strength To Go Through", I needed to have it arranged musically, so I went to Bob because he was like a father to me, like in the song "Joseph". I felt that nobody could assist me better than going to him. Maybe there was others that I could go to but I went to him.

MLW: Did the closeness between you and Bob sustain itself throughout as his popularity increased, and his presence was called on more? Was he still accessible?

JM: He was accessible, but then you didn't want to burden him. He was really accessible anytime. He is a man that was always occupied. If not talking to people, reasoning with his children. Midnight you go to his room and you would think that he's asleep, he is with his guitar. If you go there 4 o'clock in the morning and you feel that he's asleep, he's with his guitar. So you say, well, what time has this man really got for me? So if you have any little problem, not that I think that he is incapable of solving it but I wouldn't want to overburden him. And as you said, as the popularity increased, a lot more people was coming to him. I didn't feel it necessary to go to him and furthermore, my spiritual intuition, my inspiration, it started to develop too, and then you know that it is not everything you can just expect somebody to solve for you.

MLW: So why do you think that consideration was so absent in other people? Some people didn't seem to have any discretion, just in terms of his time. He seemed to be saturated by their needs and wants. Did you personally want to guard the door, maybe not literally, but to protect him because he was always being pursued?

JM: Well, we always tried to do that on the tour but he always had time for people and he is always willing to deal with the people any time. And even if he's tired, he would not show his tiredness. Sometimes you wonder if he is superhuman. He was always giving himself. I have never seen that man take any time off for himself. He's always giving. Everywhere you go people just want to see him, want to be with him. To even sit in a room with him, not even conversing at all, people just wanted to know that they are close. And if they are not talking you will find that he would be entertaining with his guitar and I guess as a Joseph, they say he is a humanitarian. He has the sort of magnetic thing inside of him that attracts people from all walks of life. I don't think it really mattered to him at all. You are there sometimes and you try to lock the door to protect him but it is what he wants.

A lot of people don't know, but we of the Twelve Tribes of Israel, we know that Bob is from the Tribe of Joseph, because he said so. He also knew so or else he wouldn't have said it, and we know that Joseph is the one that was sold by his brothers because of envy and Bob today is Joseph in the second advent. Joseph went into Egypt to restore the corn for the children in the time of famine because Joseph was a visionary man, a dreamer, and he could see more than the average man in terms of perception. Bob today has done seven albums from *Natty Dread* because that was when his career really started to herald. So is really seven albums in seven years of his career. And we know that Joseph's work in Egypt was for the seven years of famine, and after seven years he had died, not of old age either, he died very young, when that work was fulfilled, that was the time that he was taken away to rest with his Father. So we know that Bob is truly Joseph reincarnated. In this time it wasn't really corn, physical corn, it was food to uplift the minds of the people. So even with him being gone from the physical scene of action, we know that we have seven albums left behind which is our food for survival. And we know with that potency we have in our diet we can never starve ■

> "*E*verywhere you go, people just want to see him, want to be with him . . . people just wanted to know that they are close . . ."

'FAMILY MAN'...

Bob with "Family Man" and Junior Marvin in Nassau—the final leg of the 1979 World Tour.

ASTON "FAMILYMAN" BAR-RETT'S position in the Wailers is depended on, like the hands of a clock. As bassist for the group, sound synchronizer and founding member, he has contributed a solid musical background (along with brother Carlton Barrett, drummer) that has given the group an undisputed edge. A man of few words, he prefers to speak through his instrument, but had these reflections to offer.

AFB: I'm the kind of musician that I train myself to deal with certain basics, certain dimensions that fit in anywhere. When we and Bob come together, there was no set thing, we created toward that which you see here [the music].

MLW: What early indication did you get when working with the Wailers, as they became internationally known, that this was not just another group? Was there any spiritual feeling?

AFB: Well at a time, each individual will tell you something similar, but before I even started with the Wailers, I have a feeling even before I approached

my instrument. The meditation that I have, I value. And the way I meditate I know that within a time I [was destined] to meet up some bredren who were similar, not directly like me, you know, who carry through a works, and as time go by, it manifest. I can see a naturality. Some people would call it miracle *[laughter]*.

MLW: When some of the songs were coming, did you work with Bob individually or always with the group as you were trying out new things?

AFB: All forms.

MLW: Would you say that you had room to develop what was Fams' sound vibration?

AFB: You see, each different track, a different track. Each version a version. Different ways and means. If one approach you with a ways, you come with means. If one approach you with a means you come with the ways *[laughter]*.

MLW: You once mentioned about the mind being together in terms of your relationship with Bob. How do you personally reconcile things when the light shines on that particular space on stage and though the spirit is there, the physical form is not? How do you deal with that?

AFB: As you say, it's not there but it is there. But things go on. No one really expected [what happened to Bob]. Every man must work, still.

MLW: Would you say all of the Wailers are as committed to remaining together as always?

AFB: It's the best choice they got.

MLW: Have you received any outside offers?

AFB: Well, we not looking to work off no contract right now, if anything we work with the same people who we work with [Tuff Gong].

MLW: Is there something deep inside that you wish to share with people on your feelings towards Bob?

AFB: That kinda difficult. To get that feeling it come like me would have to travel through a time barrier.

MLW: As a person who is obviously able to deal with the realities of life, you know inside every man's chest beats a heart, but I guess I can appreciate what you mean about the time barrier. Is there anything that worries you?

AFB: Yeah. When things are not right. I deal with what is truth and righteousness. When things not right and your conscience is not right, then of course it's your conscience that make it not right.

"I know I was born with a price on my head . . ."
(Bob Marley)

CHAPTER 12

THE LEGACY

Just like a tree planted . . . by the river of water
That bringeth forth . . . fruits in due season
Everything in life got its purpose
Find its reason in every season, forever yeah!

("Forever Loving Jah")

AND SO, what have we got left? What gifts has Bob Marley bestowed upon us? There are so many. Joseph is a fruitful bough. Marley's songs have helped to erase the lie of inferiority which was branded on the black consciousness by racist oppressors. Black people are now more aware, and more proud, of their past. "We are who we are"— so simply put, and yet so explicit. It is a challenge to deal with the self, after which all else can be improved. Marley motivated his listeners to reject prejudicial negativism resolutely and to get up and stand up for *our* story and not the misrepresented *his*tory. Marley's musical watering will maintain the necessary moisture at the roots so that those who are guided by his words will cease to be stems and branches just blowing in the wind. He leaves a foundation that, like the pyramids, can only be marvelled at and wondered about, and leaned on without fear of their shifting. He

leaves us the impetus to examine our own psyche outside of the descriptions handed us by the "pigmentational perverts"—the parasites—in society.

> **The stone that the builder refuse**
> **Shall be the head cornerstone**
> **And no matter what games they play**
> **There is something they could never take away**

("Ride Natty Ride")

As a social activist, his lyrics leave an indelible mark on our past, present and future struggles to embrace a harmonious existence within the brotherhood and sisterhood of man on this earth. His chorus and reprise touch the circumstance of everyone, irrespective of colour, race or creed. It is mansong. Whether predicting the peril that is to come unless we change our path to one of righteousness, or promising a perfect day, he touches us all.

The songs of Bob Marley remain an eternal flame to light the way out of darkness and into a brighter and renewed consciousness. They will always be a steadfast companion to man, with ready reminders to safeguard all that upholds righteousness.

Marley will be revered as one whose luminous glow shone in the universal spreading of Rastafari, as a spiritual catalyst, who prompted new converts with his songs. His musical pronouncements strengthened the validity of Rastafari as a foundation of ideals and principles, the adherence to which has united seekers of truth, justice and equality the world over. He must be recognized as a vital energy source committed to achieving the protection and respect due to a way of life that seeks nothing more than to be at one with creation. By wearing the banner of Rastafari, Bob Marley has forced a reluctant international society to recognize it as being beyond the narrow and insular definition of cult or sect; rather, as a world community of brothers and sisters who put their trust in a heritage they can rightfully trace.

Marley has inspired, awakened and aroused that innate rebel spirit that has too long been dormant in too many of us, and incited it to fight for our survival. His songs point the way out of this involuntary exile and towards a place where we will be allowed simply to live. Marley's true legacy will be realized when the world becomes, as Thoreau once said, like the grass which confesses the influence of the slightest dew that falls on it.

Bob Marley's omnipresence is vividly depicted in what is felt to be the most poignant, most cherished, of all his compositions: "Redemption Song".

Apostle, shaman, prophet, priest, poet: call him what you will, Bob Marley lives in all of us.

"Old pirates yes they rob I
Sold I to the merchant ships
Minutes after they took I
From the bottomless pit
But my hand was made strong
By the hand of the Almighty
We forward in this generation
    triumphantly
All I ever had is songs of freedom
Won't you help to sing these songs
    of freedom
'Cause all I ever had redemption songs
Redemption songs
Emancipate yourselves from
    mental slavery
None but ourselves can free our mind
Have no fear for atomic energy
Cause none of them can stop the time
How long shall they kill our prophets
While we stand aside and look
Some say it's just a part of it
We've got to fulfill the book."

(Redemption Song)

"Every time I
    hear
The crack of
    the whip
My blood runs
    cold
I remember
On the slave
    ship
How they
    brutalised my
    very soul."
(Slave Driver)

Psalm 38

O LORD, rebuke me not in thy wrath: neither chasten me in thy hot displeasure.

2 For thine arrows stick fast in me, and thy hand presseth me sore.

3 There is no soundness in my flesh because of thine anger; neither is there any rest in my bones because of my sin.

4 For mine iniquities are gone over mine head: as an heavy burden they are too heavy for me.

5 My wounds stink and are corrupt because of my foolishness.

6 I am troubled; I am bowed down greatly; I go mourning all the day long.

7 For my loins are filled with a loathsome disease: and there is no soundness in my flesh.

8 I am feeble and sore broken: I have roared by reason of the disquietness of my heart.

9 Lord, all my desire is before thee; and my groaning is not hid from thee.

10 My heart panteth, my strength faileth me: as for the light of mine eyes, it also is gone from me.

11 My lovers and my friends stand aloof from my sore; and my kinsmen stand afar off.

12 They also that seek after my life lay snares for me: and they that seek my hurt speak mischievous things, and imagine deceits all the day long.

13 But I, as a deaf man, heard not; and I was as a dumb man that openeth not his mouth.

14 Thus I was as a man that heareth not, and in whose mouth are no reproofs.

15 For in thee, O Lord, do I hope: thou wilt hear, O Lord my God.

16 For I said, Hear me, lest otherwise they should rejoice over me: when my foot slippeth, they magnify themselves against me.

17 For I am ready to halt, and my sorrow is continually before me.

18 For I will declare mine iniquity; I will be sorry for my sin.

19 But mine enemies are lively, and they are strong: and they that hate me wrongfully are multiplied.

20 They also that render evil for good are mine adversaries; because I follow the thing that good is.

21 Forsake me not, O Lord: O my God, be not far from me.

22 Make haste to help me, O Lord my salvation.

SELAH.

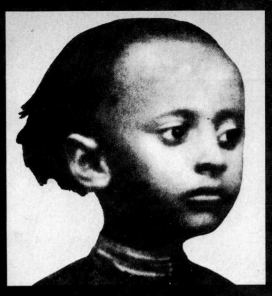

His Imperial Majesty Ras Tafari Makonnen, aged 7; descendant of King Menelik, son of King Solomon and the Queen of Sheba

The Ethiopian International Anthem

Ethiopia the land of our father,
The land where all Gods and Goddesses
    love to be.
As a swift cloud of might, so they gather,
God's children are gathered to thee.

With our Red, Gold and Green floating
    o'er us,
With our Emperor to shield us from wrong,
With our God and our future before us
We hail and we shout and we sing sweet
    songs.

CHORUS:
God bless our Negus, Negus high,
And keep Ethiopia free,
To advance with truth and right,
To advance with love and light.
With righteousness set speeding we haste to
    the call,
Humanity is pleasing, one God for us all.

Ethiopians: The tyrant is falling,
Who smote thee upon our knee,
And thy children are lustily calling,
From over the distant sea.

O Eternal God of this age,
Grant unto us a son that leads,
Thy wisdom, knowledge, understanding,
    thou gave to the sages
When Israel was so in need.

Thy voice through the dim pass has spoken,
Ethiopia shall stretch forth her hand.
By thee all barriers be broken,
And heaven bless our dear mother land.

*This was Ethiopia's national anthem before the revolution.

Now you get what you want
Do you want more
You think it's
the end
but
it's
just
the
b

"The Lion of Judah
shall break every chain
and give us the victory
again and again."

MALiKA Lee WhiTNEy

is a multi-media journalist who writes on topics relating to the arts and entertainment. Her work has appeared in magazines from *Africa Woman* to *Unique New York* and she is a regular contributor to the Jamaica Daily News and Sunday Sun in a weekly column called "Lee Lines" and "Tracks". Ms. Whitney has had a long association in the electronic media beginning with CBS TV News where she was a Researcher. She is Artistic Director of the "Pickney Players", a Children's Theatre Company which she founded in Jamaica; she is also an actress and director. A partner with Pix & Promo Public Relations Consultants, she is currently Presenter and Producer of two programmes designed for radio, "Disc Dawta" and "Sound Reasoning". Ms. Whitney has a teenaged son. She was born in Harlem, New York City, U.S.A. of Jamaican parentage.

DERMOTT hussey

is a graduate of the London Film School, and is the winner of several awards for his outstanding documentaries. He is Producer and Presenter of the television programme "Nommo" and the radio show "The Rhythm Section"— both with the Jamaica Broadcasting Corporation.

TROy CAiNE

is a designer of extensive versatility and has over fifteen years' experience in the graphics, advertising and public relations fields. He was born in the parish of St. Elizabeth, Jamaica, educated at Munro College, and briefly attended the Jamaica School of Art—where he now serves as a member on the Board of Management. Mr Caine, who now freelances, worked with the advertising firm of Lindo, Norman Craig & Kummel Limited, in Kingston for over twelve years. In 1968 he was the winner of the Human Rights Stamp Design Competition in commemoration of Human Rights Year in Jamaica. Among his works in book designing are *Alexander Bustamante—Portrait of A Hero* by Rt. Hon. Hugh Shearer; *Detained* by Pearnel Charles; and *Caribbean Cocktails & Mixed Drinks* by Mike Henry.